TABLE OF CONTENTS

2 Timothy 2:15

Be diligent to present yourself approved to God, a worker who does not need to be ashamed, rightly dividing the word of truth. NKJV

The body of Christ loves the Lord, yet so many in the body do not know who they are, what they are, or what they believe. Ignorance has saturated the saints of Christ. We can shout, we can dance, but the majority of Christians cannot give a reason for why they believe the Bible is true.

The passion of this text is to empower the sons and daughters of faith through knowledge of the Word of God, so that when all the shaking is done, they are still standing. I challenge you to read, study and then re-digest this book over and over again so that you will KNOW who you are in Jesus, and your purpose on this planet.

Thank you for investing in your spirit man! Your investment will bring stability to your spirit, soul and body, and you will reap a HUGE harvest in your everyday walk with Jesus.

Get ready! Pull out your napkin and utensils, it's time to EAT!

I would like to thank some people who helped to make this happen. My loving wife Rhonda,and my family have sacrificed many hours of my time so this could be penned. I would also like to thank Dr. Keith Johnson for pushing and encouraging me to finish this book. A special thank you to Pastor Mary Edlin and Evangelist Ted Shuttlesworth for your years of speaking into my life and teaching me so I could teach others. I would also like to thank Nicole Blackman for editing the text, and Multimedia Productions of Corning, NY for printing. This is not one person's work, but the collection of so many individuals who made Volume 2 of **TRUTH: Rock Solid Faith** come to fruition.

With sincere love,

Dr. Micheal J. Spencer

CHAPTER 1

THE BIBLE

Understanding that the Bible is not just another book on the shelf is very important. Other religions have their bible, so what makes our Bible any better, or more the Word of God than theirs? This is a good and very important question. God has answers that will enable you not to merely have blind faith.

Many think that in order to believe the Bible, you have to hang your brain on the hat rack and walk away; that is not true at all! Believing in the Bible is a very intellectual choice, not of ignorance, but of validation.

There are 66 books in the Bible

➤ There are 39 books that make up the Old Testament.

   ○ The Pentateuch (meaning 5)

      ▪ Genesis

      ▪ Exodus

      ▪ Leviticus

      ▪ Numbers

      ▪ Deuteronomy

   ○ The Historical books

      ▪ Joshua & Melanie Fuksman Judges

      ▪ Ruth

      ▪ First and Second Samuel

      ▪ First and Second Kings

      ▪ First and Second Chronicles

      ▪ Ezra

      ▪ Nehemiah

      ▪ Esther

- The books of Wisdom
    - Job
    - Psalms
    - Proverbs
    - Ecclesiastes
    - Song of Solomon
- The Major Prophets
    - Isaiah
    - Jeremiah
    - Lamentations
    - Ezekiel
    - Daniel
- The Minor Prophets
    - Hosea
    - Joel
    - Amos
    - Obadiah
    - Jonah
    - Micah
    - Nahum
    - Habakkuk
    - Zephaniah
    - Haggai
    - Zechariah
    - Malachi

➢ There are 27 books collected to make up the New Testament
- The Gospels

- Matthew
- Mark
- Luke
- John

- There is only one book that deals with the introduction of the New Testament Church
  - Acts

- The Epistles written by Paul the Apostle
  - Romans
  - First and Second Corinthians
  - Galatians
  - Ephesians
  - Philippians
  - Colossians
  - First and Second Thessalonians
  - First and Second Timothy
  - Titus
  - Philemon
  - Hebrews
    - (Whether Paul actually wrote the book of Hebrews is debated. It has his style, but the writer is never identified, so there is question of who the author is. Most scholars attribute it to Paul.)

- Epistles
  - James
  - First and Second Peter
  - First and Second John
  - Jude

- The Revelatory book

- The book of Revelation

The Bible is different to any other book on the planet

- It took 1600 years to write the Word of God
- There were 40 authors
  - The authors came from different lifestyles and backgrounds
    - Moses – trained up in Egyptian schools
    - David – shepherd
    - Luke – doctor
    - Matthew – tax collector
    - Paul – very educated man in the law
  - The authors wrote during diverse times
    - Peace
    - War
    - In victory
    - In defeat
- The Bible was written on three continents
  - Africa
  - Asia
  - Europe
- The Bible was written in three languages
  - Hebrew
  - Greek
  - Aramaic
- It was written on:
  - Papyrus
    - This was created from the papyrus plant. It is a reed that grows in shallow lakes and rivers. It was sent through the port of Byblos in mass quantities for the world to be able to write on. The actual

Greek word for books comes from the name of the port in which it was shipped, and the English word for paper is derived from the Greek word paper.

- The plant was cut in the lengths, beaten, layered and then dried. The surface after it dried was polished with a stone to make it smooth.

○ Animal skins

- They would dry skins and then shave them to get the hide thin enough, yet not too thin to write on.

- Some skins were dyed purple

○ The hard surfaced material

- Stones

- Clay

- Pottery

○ How can the Bible be accurate since it has been translated so many times?

- A manuscript is a copy of the original

- In the times of Jesus there were these individuals called Scribes. The job of a Scribe was to translate one manuscript to another. They took this very seriously. Their quest for accuracy prompted them to not only translate word to word, but from letter to letter and punctuation to punctuation. An example of this is if you were translating "hello", it would go like this, "H", "H", "E", "E", and so on until the word was complete and the punctuation was concluded.

- Because of this we have about 25,000 manuscripts of the New Testament alone in many languages! The most original manuscripts of any writing in all history.

Historical and Archeological Proof

➢ There have been many Archeological findings that prove that the Bible is historically valid.

- ○ "The discovery of the Ebla archive in northern Syria in the 1970s has shown the Biblical writings concerning the Patriarchs to be viable. Documents written on clay tablets from around 2300 B.C. demonstrate that personal and place names in the Patriarchal accounts are genuine. The name "Canaan" was in use in Ebla, a name critics once said was not used at that time and was used incorrectly in the early chapters of the Bible. The word *tehom* ("the deep") in Genesis 1:2 was said to be a late word demonstrating the late writing of the creation story. "Tehom" was part of the vocabulary at Ebla, in use some 800 years before Moses. Ancient customs reflected in the stories of the Patriarchs have also been found in clay tablets from Nuzi and Mari." *http://www.christiananswers.net/q-abr/abr-a008.html*

- ○ "The Hittites were once thought to be a Biblical legend, until their capital and records were discovered at Bogazkoy, Turkey." *http://www.christiananswers.net/q-abr/abr-a008.html*

- ○ "Many thought the Biblical references to Solomon's wealth were greatly exaggerated. Recovered records from the past show that wealth in antiquity was concentrated with the king and Solomon's prosperity was entirely feasible." *http://www.christiananswers.net/q-abr/abr-a008.html*

- ○ "It was once claimed there was no Assyrian king named Sargon as recorded in Isaiah 20:1, because this name was not known in any other record. Then, Sargon's palace was discovered in Khorsabad, Iraq. The very event mentioned in Isaiah 20, his capture of Ashdod, was recorded on the palace walls. What is more, fragments of a stela memorializing the victory were found at Ashdod itself." *http://www.christiananswers.net/q-abr/abr-a008.html*

- ○ "Another king who was in doubt was Belshazzar, king of Babylon, named in Daniel 5. The last king of Babylon was Nabonidus according to recorded history. Tablets were found showing that Belshazzar was Nabonidus' son who served as coregent in Babylon. Thus, Belshazzar could offer to make Daniel "third highest ruler in the kingdom" (Dan. 5:16) for reading the handwriting on the wall, the highest available position. Here we see the "eye-witness" nature of the Biblical record, as is so often brought out by the discoveries of archaeology." *http://www.christiananswers.net/q-abr/abr-a008.html*

- ○ The most documented Biblical event is the world-wide flood described in Genesis 6-9. A number of Babylonian documents have been discovered which describe the same flood. *http://www.christiananswers.net/q-abr/abr-a008.html*

- The Sumerian King List…lists kings who reigned for long periods of time. Then a great flood came. Following the flood, Sumerian kings ruled for much shorter periods of time. This is the same pattern found in the Bible. Men had long life spans before the flood and shorter life spans after the flood. The 11th tablet of the Gilgamesh Epic speaks of an ark, animals taken on the ark, birds sent out during the course of the flood, the ark landing on a mountain, and a sacrifice offered after the ark landed. *http://www.christiananswers.net/q-abr/abr-a008.html*

- Sumerian tablets record the confusion of language as we have in the Biblical account of the Tower of Babel (Genesis 11:1-9). There was a golden age when all mankind spoke the same language. Speech was then confused by the god Enki, lord of wisdom. The Babylonians had a similar account in which the gods destroyed a temple tower and "scattered them abroad and made strange their speech." *http://www.christiananswers.net/q-abr/abr-a008.html*

- We have tangible evidence placing Abraham in these locations at the time stated. A discovery made in 1975 in the ancient city of Ebla **(4)**, yielded 17,000 clay tablets. Ebla was a powerful city in what is now Syria, in the region between Mesopotamia and Palestine. On these tablets, a number of names are recorded, including Isaac, Jacob, and Abraham, as well as the names of Abraham's father, grandfather and great grandfather, Terah, Nahor and Serug. These names are also known from other sources in Northwest Mesopotamia in both Babylonian and Old Assyrian texts. *http://www.suite101.com/lesson.cfm/18327/1589*

The Eye Witness of Jesus

- ➢ The disciples and many other individuals who wrote about Him and saw Him.

  - The disciples wrote the first 4 books of the New Testament

  - In I Corinthians 15:3-8, *For I delivered unto you first of all that which I also received, how that Christ died for our sins according to the scriptures;* *4And that he was buried, and that he rose again the third day according to the scriptures: 5And that he was seen of Cephas, then of the twelve: 6After that, he was seen of above five hundred brethren at once; of whom the greater part remain unto this present, but some are fallen asleep. 7After that, he was seen of James; then of all the apostles. 8And last of all he was seen of me also, as of one born out of due time. KJV*

Many have tried to disprove the Bible but with research found that they could no longer deny its validity.

- o Simon Greenleaf

  - One of the founding fathers of Harvard

  - He was not a believer, and during one of his class sessions as he was speaking against Christianity, a student asked if he had researched the historical evidence of Jesus.

  - He began to research and came to the historical conclusion that proofs demand that the life and resurrection of Jesus cannot be denied.

  - The book he wrote is available online for free

    - http://www.law.umkc.edu/faculty/projects/ftrials/jesus/greenleaf.html

  - Dr. Greenleaf concluded after much study to disprove the resurrection that according to jurisdiction of legal evidence the resurrection of Jesus Christ was the best supported event in all of history.

- o Josh McDowell

  - He went out to prove that the Bible was a lie and from the evidences that he found had to become a believer. He debates in the Ivy League Colleges the facts of the Bible.

    - His book is entitled, *More Evidence that Demands Verdict*. I encourage you to purchase this book for your reference.

- o Non Christian writers like the Jewish historian Josephus

  - Josephus was not a Christian historian, yet he documents Jesus Christ as a valid historical person and writes about Jesus in two different chapters of his book.

The Bible is proven to be prophetic.

- ➤ Interesting facts of the prophetic truths that Jesus is the Messiah

  - o "That the **entire lineage of the coming Messiah was foretold 2069 years before** he was even born.

  - o The **city he would be born in – 726 years in advance** (Micah)

  - o He would **minister in Galilee – 763 years in advance** (Isaiah)

- The **year and day that Jesus would enter into Jerusalem** as a king just prior to his arrest and crucifixion – **515 years in advance** (Daniel)

- **He would die on a cross** – **1012 years in advance** (Psalms) (before this was a known execution mode)

- He would be **betrayed for 30 pieces of silver** – **512 years in advance** (Zechariah)

- Soldiers would **cast lots for his clothing** – **1012 years in advance** (Psalms)

- That he would **rise from the dead** – **1012 years in advance** (Psalms)"
  http://students.syr.edu/scf/docs/Fulfilled%20Prophecies%20of%20Christ.pdf

- Just a few of the 300 prophetic words spoken about Jesus in the Old Testament and fulfilled in the New Testament.

  - That Jesus would be born in Bethlehem

    - OT – Micah 5:2

    - NT – Matthew 2:3

  - Jesus would be born of a virgin

    - OT – Isaiah 7:14

    - NT – Matthew 1; Luke 1

  - Come from the seed of a woman, not of man

    - OT – Genesis 3:15

    - NT – Matthew 1

  - He would enter Jerusalem riding a donkey

    - OT – Zechariah 9:9

    - NT – Matthew 21:5; Luke 19:32-37

  - He would be betrayed by a friend

    - OT – Psalms 41:9

    - NT – Matthew 27:3-10

  - Jesus would be sold for 30 pieces of silver

    - OT – Zechariah 11:12

- NT – Matthew 26:14
  - The money would be thrown to the floor
    - OT- Zechariah 11:13
    - NT – Matthew 27:5
  - The would gamble for His clothes
    - OT - Psalms 22:16
    - NT – Matthew 27:35
  - He would be pierced
    - OT – Zechariah 12:10
    - NT – John 19:34
  - Hands and feet would be pierced
    - OT – Psalms 22:16
    - NT – Galatians 3:13
  - No bones would be broken
    - OT – Psalms 34:20
    - NT – John 19:33
  - That he would declare, "My God, my God…."
    - OT – Psalms 22:1
    - NT – Matthew 27:46
  - The Messiah would be resurrected
    - OT – Psalms 16:10
    - NT – Acts 2:31
  - There are so many more, these are just a few.

Science[1]

> **Statements Consistent With Paleontology**

---

[1] The entire science section is from the website http://www.clarifyingchristianity.com/science.shtml

- Dinosaurs are referred to in several Bible books. The book of Job describes two dinosaurs. One is described in chapter 40 starting at verse 15, and the other in chapter 41 starting at verse 1. We think you will agree that 1½ chapters about dinosaurs is a lot—since most people do not even realize that they are mentioned in the Bible. (Actually *reading* the Bible would help, though.)

➢ **Statements Consistent With Astronomy**

- The Bible frequently refers to the great number of stars in the heavens. Here <u>are two examples.</u>

  - <u>Genesis 22:17; Jeremiah 33:22</u>

  - Even today, scientists admit that they do not know how many stars there are. Only about 3,000 can be seen with the naked eye. We have seen *estimates* of 10^{21} stars—which is a lot of stars.[2] (The number of grains of sand on the earth's seashores is estimated to be 10^{25}. As scientists discover more stars, wouldn't it be interesting to discover that these two numbers match?)

  - The Bible also says that each star is unique.

    - 1 Corinthians 15:41

    - All stars look alike to the naked eye.* Even when seen through a telescope, they seem to be just points of light. However, analysis of their light spectra reveals that each is unique and different from all others.[1] (*Note: We understand that people can perceive some slight difference in color and apparent brightness when looking at stars with the naked eye, but we would not expect a person living in the first century A.D. to claim they differ from one another.)

  - The Bible describes the precision of movement in the universe.

    - Jeremiah 31:35,36

- The Bible describes the suspension of the Earth in space.

  - Job 26:7

> **Statements Consistent With Meteorology**

- The Bible describes the circulation of the atmosphere.

  - Ecclesiastes 1:6

- The Bible includes some principles of fluid dynamics.

  - Job 28:25

    - The fact that air has *weight* was proven scientifically only about 300 years ago. The relative weights of air and water are needed for the efficient functioning of the world's hydrologic cycle, which in turn sustains life on the earth.[1] (If you are a physics enthusiast, please ignore our omission of the terms mass, gravity, and density from this comment.)

> **Statements Consistent With Biology**

- The book of Leviticus (written prior to 1400 BC) describes the value of blood.

  - Leviticus 17:11

    - The blood carries water and nourishment to every cell, maintains the body's temperature, and removes the waste material of the body's cells. The blood also carries oxygen from the lungs throughout the body. In 1616, William Harvey discovered that blood circulation is the key factor in physical life—confirming what the Bible revealed 3,000 years earlier.[1]

- The Bible describes biogenesis (the development of living organisms from other living organisms) and the stability of each kind of living organism.

- Genesis 1:11,12; Genesis 1:21; Genesis 1:25

  - The phrase "according to its kind" occurs repeatedly, stressing the reproductive integrity of each kind of animal and plant. Today we know this occurs because all of these reproductive systems are programmed by their genetic codes.[1]

o The Bible describes the chemical nature of flesh.

- Genesis 2:7; Genesis 3:19

o It is a proven fact that a person's mental and spiritual health is strongly correlated with physical health.[1] The Bible revealed this to us with these statements (and others) written by King Solomon about 950 BC.

- Proverbs 12:4; Proverbs 14:30; Proverbs 15:30; Proverbs 16:24; Proverbs 17:22

➤ **Statements Consistent With Anthropology**

o We have cave paintings and other evidence that people inhabited caves. The Bible also describes cave men.

- Job 30:5,6

  - Note that these were not ape-men, but descendants of those who scattered from Babel. They were driven from the community by those tribes who competed successfully for the more desirable regions of the earth. Then for some reason they deteriorated mentally, physically, and spiritually. [1] (Go into a bad part of your town and you will see this concept in action today.)

➤ **Statements Consistent With Hydrology**

o The bible includes reasonably complete descriptions of the hydrologic cycle.[3]

- Psalm 135:7; Jeremiah 10:13

  - In these verses you can see several phases of the hydrologic cycle—the worldwide processes of evaporation, translation aloft by atmospheric circulation, condensation with electrical discharges, and precipitation.[1]

- Job 36:27-29

  - This simple verse has remarkable scientific insight. The drops of water which eventually pour down as rain first become vapor and then condense to tiny liquid water droplets in the clouds. These finally coalesce into drops large enough to overcome the updrafts that suspend them in the air.[1]

- Hydrothermal vents[4] are described in two books of the Bible written before 1400BC—more than 3,000 years before their discovery by science.

  - Genesis 7:11; Job 38:16

> **Statements Consistent With Geology**

- The Bible describes the Earth's crust (along with a comment on astronomy).

  - Jeremiah 31:37

    - Although some scientists claim that they have now measured the size of the universe, it is interesting to note that every human attempt to drill through the earth's crust to the plastic mantle beneath has, thus far, ended in failure.[1]

- The Bible described the shape of the earth centuries before people thought that the earth was spherical.

  - Isaiah 40:22

- The word translated "circle" here is the Hebrew word chuwg which is also translated "circuit," or "compass" (depending on the context). That is, it indicates something spherical, rounded, or arched—not something that is flat or square.

  The book of Isaiah was written sometime between 740 and 680 BC. This is at least 300 years before Aristotle suggested that the earth might be a sphere in this book *On the Heavens*.

  This brings up an important historical note related to this topic. Many people are aware of the conflict between Galileo and the Roman Catholic Pope, Paul V. After publishing *A Dialogue on the Two Principal Systems of the World*, Galileo was summoned to Rome, where he was forced to renounce his findings. (At that time, "theologians" of the Roman Catholic Church maintained that the Earth was the center of the universe, and to assert otherwise was deemed heretical.)

  We could not find any place in the Bible that claims that the Earth is flat, or that it is the center of the universe. History shows that this conflict, which took place at the time of the Inquisition, was part of a power struggle. As a result, scientific *and* biblical knowledge became casualties—an effect we still feel to this day.

➤ Statements Consistent With Physics

- The Bible suggests the presence of nuclear processes like those we associate with nuclear weaponry. This is certainly not something that could have been explained in 67 AD using known scientific principles (when Peter wrote the following verse).

  - 2 Peter 3:10

    - The Bible contains passages that describe something like television—something that allows everyone on earth see a single event. (Note: such passages typically refer to the end of time. It may not be long before *all* of us learn *for sure* whether the Bible is true or not.)

References

[1] *The DEFENDER'S Study Bible*, Word Publishing, Grand Rapids, Michigan (1995).
[2] http://imagine.gsfc.nasa.gov/docs/ask_astro/answers/970115.html
[3] http://ww2010.atmos.uiuc.edu/(Gh)/guides/mtr/hyd/smry.rxml
[4] http://www.ceoe.udel.edu/extreme2004/geology/hydrothermalvents/index.html

CHAPTER 1 CONTINUED
The Bible

There are different ways to read and study the Bible. In this chapter we are going to teach you how to read, and how to study the Bible. We are also going to lay the foundations by teaching you some basic truths for understanding the Bible.

HERMENEUTICS

I. 2 Timothy 2:15, *Be diligent to present yourself approved to God, a worker who does not need to be ashamed, rightly dividing the word of truth. NKJV*

    A. The term, hermeneutics simply means how to interpret the Bible correctly.

    B. There is a need to understand how to correctly interpret the Word of God.

    C. There are two types of interpretation of the Scripture:

        1. Historico Grammatico Exegesis

            a. We take history and grammar and find out what the original writer was saying in that portion of Scripture.

            b. Easier explained – Literal interpretation

                (1) What the original writer wrote under this inspiration of the Holy Spirit is what we are striving to know.

        2. Spiritualization

            a. This means that even though the original writer meant red, you and I can make it mean yellow because we do not like or would rather it be yellow.

            b. Easier explained – It can mean what you desire it to mean.

                (1) It does not matter what the original purpose of the truth being taught, if you want it to mean something different you can read into the verse and make it say what you want.

                (2) These are the groups that make the Bible fit their agenda and purpose and they use the Bible for their

own convenience rather than living by the Word of God to shape their lives.

D. We are literal interpreters.

1. We believe that God spoke to and through the men who wrote the Word of God and that what the Father wanted us to know, He had the pen.

    a. LITERALLY, NOT FIGURITIVELY

2. 2 Peter 2:20-21, *knowing this first, that no prophecy of Scripture is of any private interpretation, 21for prophecy never came by the will of man, but holy men of God spoke as they were moved by the Holy Spirit. NKJV*

3. I Thessalonians 2:13, *For this reason we also thank God without ceasing, because when you received the word of God which you heard from us, you welcomed it not as the word of men, but as it is in truth, the word of God, which also effectively works in you who believe. NKJV*

4. 2 Timothy 3:16-17, *All Scripture is given by inspiration of God, and is profitable for doctrine, for reproof, for correction, for instruction in righteousness, 17that the man of God may be complete, thoroughly equipped for every good work. NKJV*

READING THE BIBLE

II. Reading the Bible daily is very important because it feeds your spiritual man.

A. The Word of God is living and builds your spiritual man.

1. Hebrews 4:12, *For the word of God is **living and powerful**, and sharper than any two-edged sword, piercing even to the division of soul and spirit, and of joints and marrow, and is a discerner of the thoughts and intents of the heart. NKJV*

2. John 6:63, *It is the Spirit who gives life; the flesh profits nothing. **The words that I speak to you are spirit, and they are life**. NKJV*

B. Jesus is the Word that became flesh

1. John 1:1, *In the beginning was the Word, and the Word was with God, and the Word was God. NKJV*

2. John 1:14, *And the Word became flesh and dwelt among us, and we beheld His glory, the glory as of the only begotten of the Father, full of grace and truth. NKJV*

a. As we are reading the Bible, we are spiritually eating Jesus and learning who He and the Father are, and what they desire for us.

b. Your spirit and faith get fed as you read the Bible daily.

(1) Romans 10:17, *So then faith comes by hearing, and hearing by the word of God. NKJV*

c. The more you read the Bible or hear the Word of God, the quicker your grow in Him and your faith in Jesus will grow.

III. When we begin reading the Bible we need to approach it in a different manner to reading just any another book.

   A. When reading the Bible, read with the mindset of, "What is Daddy teaching me about Himself today?" or, "What is Jesus teaching me about myself that will help me be more like Him?"

   B. When reading the Word like this daily, you will start having the Holy Spirit reveal who your Daddy is and how He desires you to live for Him.

    1. GREAT READING BIBLES

      a. One of the best Bibles to read is called the MESSAGE BIBLE.

      b. This Bible is made for reading not for studying.

      c. It is in everyday language and keeps the Bible in letter form so you can grasp the whole meaning of the original writer and be able to apply it to your life with Jesus today.

      d. A good place to buy this Bible is at www.cbd.com

      e. NEW KING JAMES BIBLE

      f. NEW INTERNATIONAL BIBLE

      g. AMPLIFIED BIBLE

      h. These are all good reading Bibles to take out all the 'thee's' and 'thou's' so you can understand. They are translated in today's language.

    2. WHERE DO I BEGIN?

      a. Do not begin at the beginning!

        (1) You will get bored or confused.

  b. Begin reading the book of St. John (the 4th book of the New Testament). This book teaches how much Jesus loves you and what He did to buy you back from sin.

    (1) Then go to the Book of James (this is a very practical book)

    (2) Then go back to the beginning of the New Testament and start reading in Matthew and go all the way through.

STUDYING THE BIBLE

IV. Studying the Bible is much different than just reading.

 A. There are many ways to study the Bible and many tools that will help you on the way.

 B. It used to be that if you did not have a library worth thousands or knew Greek and Hebrew that you would not be able to understand well.

 C. Thank Jesus for the internet!!

  1. www.e-sword.net is a Bible program available on the internet that is worth thousands of dollars for FREE! Yes, I said, FREE!

   a. Just go and download the Bibles, commentaries and dictionaries and you will have library right in your computer that will help you study the Bible.

V. A GREAT STUDY BIBLE

 A. I always suggest the New Spirit Filled Life Bible and encourage people to buy it at www.cbd.com. It is best read in the New King James Version of the Bible. It is the study Bible that I use and preach out of each week.

VI. How do I study?

 A. There are a few ways to study

  1. The first is called a topical study

   b. When you choose a topic in the Bible or something you are dealing with and then study it all through the Bible to find what God is saying about it.

    ○ Vine's Expository – this book deals with topics and can be acquired through the e-sword for a small cost.

    ○ Strong's Exhaustive Concordance – this book is free and included in the e-sword package. This book will tell you every single time a word is used in the Bible and where it is an what the exact definition.

- The Harmony of the Gospels

    a. One time I wanted to study Jesus and how He thought and reacted in every situation. So I opened my Spirit Filled Life Bible and between the Old and New Testaments is a study opportunity called the 'Harmony of the Gospels'.

    b. I literally wrote down in a notebook every verse word for word. It took a long time, but when you write something out you understand and remember it better.

- These two styles of studying are a good place to begin. It takes a little time, but coupled with other study books you will grow quickly and it is exciting to really understand more about our Daddy.

I would encourage you to read, both for study and for personal devotions all books that are written by Kenneth Hagin. They are filled with the Word and will help both in studying topics and for personal encouragement.

CHAPTER 2

Prayer

Prayer is the most powerful weapon a Christian has in their spiritual toolbox. The truth is though, that MOST Christians do not know how to pray. They do not understand, because of the lack of teaching, that there is more than one type of prayer that can be used to obtain the results they desire.

With a hammer, you cannot do the same job as you would with a screwdriver. Similarly, each type of prayer in the Word has the ability to acquire a different result. When used correctly, each type of prayer will help you get what you need in a quicker manner.

That is why we pray. We pray to get an answer! If you were not praying to get a result, then you would not pray. So we need to learn how to pray so we can get the results that we are praying to receive.

Let's begin by studying:

> ### **What Prayer is NOT**

   - There is no one-way to pray.

   - Prayer from the heart is what our Father desires from us.

   - It is not:

      - **Pompous**

         - Starting prayer with all the thee's and thou's, using all the big words

      - **Competitive**

         - Praying a prayer and then waiting for someone to top it

      - **Chanting**

         - Having someone say the same thing, over and over and over

      - **Yelling**

         - God isn't deaf

         - It is not a screaming match

         - It is not more powerful if it is louder

- **Spooky**
  - Start talking to a parent as their child in a spooky religious manner

> ***Prayer is from the heart***

- Sharing what you feel and desire

- All types of prayer must come from this one major truth

- If it is not from the heart, and sincere, then it is bogus!

> **The Different Types of PRAYER**

- o **Positions of prayer:**

  - Kneeling

    - Psalms 95:6, *Oh come, let us worship and bow down; Let us kneel before the Lord our Maker. NKJV*

    - Ephesians 3:14-17, *For this reason I bow my knees to the Father of our Lord Jesus Christ, [15]from whom the whole family in heaven and earth is named, [16]that He would grant you, according to the riches of His glory, to be strengthened with might through His Spirit in the inner man, [17]that Christ may dwell in your hearts through faith; that you, being rooted and grounded in love, NKJV*

  - Laying prostrate

    - Matthew 26:39, *He went a little farther and fell on His face, and prayed, saying, "O My Father, if it is possible, let this cup pass from Me; nevertheless, not as I will, but as You will." NKJV*

  - The position of the body is not the issue

- o **Communication:** building a relationship with God

  - Getting to know Him, not just know about Him

  - Literally talking with Him and He will speak to us

  - It is a two way relationship

  - It is sharing what is really in your heart

- Daddy wants you to share everything, He knows it all anyway.

  o Share when you are happy

  o Share when you are sad

  o Share when you are mad

  o Share when you are frustrated

  o Share when you confused

  o Be honest with Him about all things

- This is building a friendship with Christ

  o John 15:15, *No longer do I call you servants, for a servant does not know what his master is doing; but I have called you friends, for all things that I heard from My Father I have made known to you. NKJV*

  o Moses was called a friend of God

    ▪ James 2:23, *And the Scripture was fulfilled which says, "Abraham believed God, and it was accounted to him for righteousness." And he was called the friend of God. NKJV*

  o God wants to have a relationship with us and that means we need to talk with Him and get to know Him through His Word, through time in prayer and in the House of God.

o **Supplication**: a humble, earnest, detailed prayer

  ▪ This tool in your toolbox is the one where you get detailed.

  ▪ Many Christians have been taught that you should just pray and be happy with what you get.

  ▪ God responds to a pure heart and when you are detailed God responds in details.

    • God is a detail God.

    • Just look at a leaf on a tree! There are so many details to the simplest of God's creation. This shows He loves and is a God of detail.

    • When you pray, be specific.

- Acts 1:14, *These all continued with one accord in prayer and supplication, with the women and Mary the mother of Jesus, and with His brothers. NKJV*

- Ephesians 6:18, *praying always with all prayer and supplication in the Spirit, being watchful to this end with all perseverance and supplication for all the saints— NKJV*

- Philippians 4:6-7, *Be anxious for nothing, but in everything by prayer and supplication, with thanksgiving, let your requests be made known to God; 7and the peace of God, which surpasses all understanding, will guard your hearts and minds through Christ Jesus. NKJV*

- BE a seeker!

  - Matthew 7:7-11, *"Ask, and it will be given to you; **seek**, and you will find; knock, and it will be opened to you. 8For everyone who asks receives, and he who seeks finds, and to him who knocks it will be opened. 9Or what man is there among you who, if his son asks for bread, will give him a stone? 10Or if he asks for a fish, will he give him a serpent? 11If you then, being evil, know how to give good gifts to your children, how much more will your Father who is in heaven give good things to those who ask Him! NKJV*

- **Intercession**: standing in the gap in prayer between God and a person(s) who has provoked judgment upon themselves.

  - Genesis 18:23-32, *And Abraham came near and said, "Would You also destroy the righteous with the wicked? 24Suppose there were fifty righteous within the city; would You also destroy the place and not spare it for the fifty righteous that were in it? 25Far be it from You to do such a thing as this, to slay the righteous with the wicked, so that the righteous should be as the wicked; far be it from You! Shall not the Judge of all the earth do right?" 26So the Lord said, "If I find in Sodom fifty righteous within the city, then I will spare all the place for their sakes." 27Then Abraham answered and said, "Indeed now, I who am but dust and ashes have taken it upon myself to speak to the Lord 28Suppose there were five less than the fifty righteous; would You destroy all of the city for lack of five?" So He said, "If I find there forty-five, I will not destroy it." 29And he spoke to Him yet again and said, "Suppose there should be forty found there?" So He said, "I will not do it for the sake of forty." 30Then he said, "Let not the Lord be angry, and I will speak: Suppose thirty should be* found there?" So He said, "I will not do it if I find thirty there." *31And he said, "Indeed now, I have taken it upon myself to speak to the Lord: Suppose twenty should be found there?" So He said, "I will not destroy it for the sake of twenty." 32Then he said, "Let not the Lord be angry, and I will speak but once more: Suppose ten should be found there?" And He said, "I will not destroy it for the sake of ten." NKJV*

- Abraham stood between God and man and interceded for the souls in Sodom. God was going to destroy, but because of Abraham God recanted and stayed the judgment, even for a time. Abraham changed history for a short period of time by interceding for the city.

▪ Psalm 106:19-23, *They made a calf in Horeb, And worshiped the molded image. 20Thus they changed their glory Into the image of an ox that eats grass. 21They forgot God their Savior, Who had done great things in Egypt, 22Wondrous works in the land of Ham, Awesome things by the Red Sea. 23Therefore He said that He would destroy them, Had not Moses His chosen one stood before Him in the breach, To turn away His wrath, lest He destroy them. NKJV*

- Moses interceded for the children of Israel when God was ready to wipe them out for their disobedience. Because Moses interceded, God relented and stepped back. Moses changed the course of history by the prayer of intercession.

▪ Ezekiel 22:30-31, *So I sought for a man among them who would make a wall, and stand in the gap before Me on behalf of the land, that I should not destroy it; but I found no one. 31Therefore I have poured out My indignation on them; I have consumed them with the fire of My wrath; and I have recompensed their deeds on their own heads," says the Lord GOD. NKJV*

- God was looking for someone to stand in the gap between man and God. Because He could not find one, judgment came upon the people.

▪ Joel 2:17, *Let the priests, who minister to the Lord, Weep between the porch and the altar; Let them say, "Spare Your people, O Lord, And do not give Your heritage to reproach, That the nations should rule over them. Why should they say among the peoples, 'Where is their God?'" NKJV*

▪ John 17 – This is the prayer of Jesus for us! He is interceding for US.

- **Prayer of Faith**:
  - Having no doubt when you pray, it will be answered.
  - Trust when you voice your petition there is no question the answer is enroute.
  - What is FAITH?
    - Hebrews 11:1 - *NOW FAITH is the assurance (the confirmation, [a]the title deed) of the things [we] hope for, being the proof of things [we] do not see and the conviction of their reality [faith perceiving as real fact what is not revealed to the senses]. AMPLIFIED BIBLE*
    - Faith is believing that you have something before you can see it manifested in this natural realm.
    - God is not moved by need, circumstances nor good will. God is moved by faith!
    - Faith is not:
      - I believe it when I see it
      - I can completely understand it so now I have it
      - Faith in Faith
    - Faith is – GOD SAID IT IN HIS WORD, IT IS TRUE, NO MATTER WHAT THE CIRCUMSTANCES DECLARE.
      - God holds His Word above His name (Ps. 138:2)
    - Faith can be measured
      - O ye of Little Faith
      - O ye of Great Faith
      - The disciples prayed – "Increase our faith"
    - <u>**So when our trust or faith in God is matured, faith coupled with the Word brings the answer through prayer!**</u>
  - John 10:10 - *The thief does not come except to **steal, and to kill, and to destroy**. I have come that they may have life, and that they may have it more abundantly.*

- We automatically think that the devil is trying to steal, kill and destroy our stuff and situation.

  - Satan does not need your job

  - Satan does not need your money

  - Satan does not need your house

  - Satan does not need your children

  - Satan does not need your health

  - Satan does not need your soul

  - Satan is actively striving to steal your FAITH.

- When we pray the prayer of faith we are receiving the answer before we can see it actually appear on this planet.

- That means we do not constantly pray for it, once you pray, you praise Him for the answer.

  - This type of prayer mainly works with things that do not have the ability to exercise personal will.

  - This is mainly used for intangible things.

    - A financial blessing

    - A healing

    - Anything that a person cannot say no!

- Don't be shaken by the circumstances, keep the faith!

  - Matthew 21:19, *So Jesus answered and said to them, "Assuredly, I say to you, if you have faith and do not doubt, you will not only do what was done to the fig tree, but also if you say to this mountain, 'Be removed and be cast into the sea,' it will be done. 22And whatever things you ask in prayer, believing, you will receive." NKJV*

- **Power of Attorney**:

  - To act on behalf of another.

  - To make decisions for someone else as if you are that person.

  - It is all in the name that is backing the account

- If I were to go to billionaire's bank, stand in line for a teller, and when it was my turn, ask for $1 million dollars from the persons account, the teller would say (politely, I hope), "Sir, I have no authority to give you those funds. I am sorry." But if I removed a check from my pocket signed by the billionaire himself, she would smile, excuse herself for a few minutes to make sure the check was authentic, verify my identity, and then give me $1 million in cash. The difference is in the authorization granted by billionaire's signature, power to transfer funds "in his name."

- Authority being passed like a baton (a relay race)

  - God has given Jesus the authority to act on His behalf while Jesus was walking on this planet.

    - Acts 10:38, *how God anointed Jesus of Nazareth with the Holy Spirit and with power, who went about doing good and healing all who were oppressed by the devil, for God was with Him. NKJV*

    - John 12:49, *For I have not spoken on My own authority; but the Father who sent Me gave Me a command, what I should say and what I should speak. NKJV*

    - Matthew 28:18, *For I have not spoken on My own authority; but the Father who sent Me gave Me a command, what I should say and what I should speak. NKJV*

    - John 5:26, *For as the Father has life in Himself, so He has granted the Son to have life in Himself, NKJV*

  - Jesus then gave us His authority to act on behalf of Him when He went to sit on the right hand of the throne of God.

    - Jesus gave us authority to act on behalf of Himself.

      - God the Father recognizes that authority because it is signed in the name of His Son.

    - Matthew 28:18-20, *And Jesus came and spoke to them, saying, "All authority has been given to Me in heaven and on earth. *19**Go** *therefore and make disciples of all the nations, baptizing them in the name of the Father and of the Son and of the Holy Spirit, *20*teaching them to observe all things that I have* *commanded you; and lo, I am with you always, even to the end of the age." Amen. NKJV*

- ○ Luke 9:1-2, *Then He called His twelve disciples together and gave them power and authority over all demons, and to cure diseases. ²He sent them to preach the kingdom of God and to heal the sick. NKJV*

- ○ John 14:10-14, *Do you not believe that I am in the Father, and the Father in Me? The words that I speak to you I do not speak on My own authority; but the Father who dwells in Me does the works. ¹¹Believe Me that I am in the Father and the Father in Me, or else believe Me for the sake of the works themselves. ¹²"Most assuredly, I say to you, he who believes in Me, the works that I do he will do also; and greater works than these he will do, because I go to My Father. ¹³And whatever you ask in My name, that I will do, that the Father may be glorified in the Son. ¹⁴If you ask anything in My name, I will do it. NKJV*

- ○ Mark 16:17-20, *And these signs will follow those who believe: In My name they will cast out demons; they will speak with new tongues; ¹⁸they will take up serpents; and if they drink anything deadly, it will by no means hurt them; they will lay hands on the sick, and they will recover." ¹⁹So then, after the Lord had spoken to them, He was received up into heaven, and sat down at the right hand of God. ²⁰And they went out and preached everywhere, the Lord working with them and confirming the word through the accompanying signs. Amen. NKJV*

- ▪ If Jesus did it here on this planet, then we can do it through Him!

- ▪ He has given us His AUTHORITY through His NAME.

- ○ **Prayer of Agreement:**

  - ▪ There is a powerful truth that if people agree and aim at something together, they create energy to accomplish a goal.

  - ▪ The devil understands what happens when people get together and believe in one direction.

    - • This is why he strives to cause DIVISION.

- o Separation has always, from the Garden of Eden, been the goal of the devil. If he can separate, then strength and synergy are lost.

- o Mark 3:24-25, *If a kingdom is divided against itself, that kingdom cannot stand. 25And if a house is divided against itself, that house cannot stand. NKJV*

- o Divide and conquer!

    - ▪ This is why he strives to strongly against marriage. Marriage is the two becoming one flesh, and moving as ONE.

- ▪ Whenever people have come together with one mind and purpose, results are assured.

    - Acts 2:1-4, *When the Day of Pentecost had fully come, they were all with one accord in one place. 2And suddenly there came a sound from heaven, as of a rushing mighty wind, and it filled the whole house where they were sitting. 3Then there appeared to them divided tongues, as of fire, and one sat upon each of them. 4And they were all filled with the Holy Spirit and began to speak with other tongues, as the Spirit gave them utterance. NKJV*

    - Acts 2:46-47, *So continuing daily with one accord in the temple, and breaking bread from house to house, they ate their food with gladness and simplicity of heart, 47praising God and having favor with all the people. And the Lord added to the church daily those who were being saved. NKJV*

    - Acts 4:31, *And when they had prayed, the place where they were assembled together was shaken; and they were all filled with the Holy Spirit, and they spoke the word of God with boldness. NKJV*

    - Whenever the children of God moved in ONENESS or AGREEMENT, they accomplished what they desired.

- ▪ Matthew 18:18-20, *"Assuredly, I say to you, whatever you bind on earth will be bound in heaven, and whatever you loose on earth will be loosed in heaven. 19"**Again I say to you that if two of you agree on earth concerning anything that they ask, it will be done for them by My Father in heaven.** 20For where two or three are gathered together in My name, I am there in the midst of them." NKJV*

- Two or more people have to come into agreement for what they are asking God to accomplish.

    o Write it down, so it is clear and everyone is on the same page. (It has to be Biblically sound)

    o Be detailed in what is expected as a result.

    o Do not change your confession or agreement no matter what the circumstances declare.

        ▪ Stand strong together. When one get's weak in faith, the other can build them up so the agreement will not be broken.

        ▪ One heart and one mind are necessary to accomplish the desired result in prayer.

o **Praise & Worship**: (See Chapter 11)

    ▪ Praise is thanking God for what He's done.

    ▪ Worship is recognizing God for who He is.

        • Praise and Worship are a massive part of prayer.

            o Psalm 100:4, *Enter into His gates with thanksgiving, And into His courts with praise. Be thankful to Him, and bless His name. NKJV*

    ▪ This is not saying that you have to have a praise and worship service before you can pray. What it means is that as you praise and worship your Father, you become more aware and focused on Him, instead of on this world.

    ▪ When you praise it stirs faith, reminding yourself what He has already accomplished and of His very nature and character. When you do this your, spirit rises with faith and adoration for Daddy.

        • Paul and Silas did this when they were in jail.

            o Acts 16:25-26, *But at midnight Paul and Silas were praying and singing hymns to God, and the prisoners were listening to them. 26Suddenly there was a great earthquake, so that the foundations of the prison were shaken; and immediately all the doors were opened and everyone's chains were loosed. NKJV*

o **Praying in the Spirit**:

- This is when the Holy Spirit prays through you when you do not know what to pray.

- There was a woman praying in her upstairs apartment and she was getting a little excited as she was praying. She was praying in tongues and the Spirit of God placed a burden on her and she began to intercede in tongues. The woman from the downstairs apartment was from Sicily and ran upstairs and knocked on her door. The lady came to the door and apologized to her neighbor if she was disturbing her. The lady from Sicily said no, you do not understand, where did you learn Italian, because you were speaking perfect Sicilian Italian about a boy drowning off the coast in Italy.

- The Holy Spirit will pray through you in tongues for things you do not know or understand. God is moved through prayer, so you become that vessel of honor for use by the King.

  - Romans 8:26, *Likewise the Spirit also helps in our weaknesses. For we do not know what we should pray for as we ought, but the Spirit Himself makes intercession for us with groanings which cannot be uttered. NKJV*

    - When you pray in tongues, the Spirit is using you as a willing vessel to pray for people or situation's that you do not know.

    - You could be praying for someone overseas or next door, a person dying or a person calling out to God for help. You could be praying for your future.

- When you pray in the Spirit you are edifying your spirit

  - I Cor. 14:4a, *He who speaks in a tongue edifies himself….. NKJV*

  - Jude 20, *But you, beloved, building yourselves up on your most holy faith, praying in the Holy Spirit, NKJV*

- When you pray in tongues you are speaking divine secrets

  - That means you are praying or worshiping God about things that no man knows.

    - I Cor. 14:2, *For he who speaks in a tongue does not speak to men but to God, for no one understands him; however, in the spirit he speaks mysteries. NKJV*

- Acts 2:11, *Cretans and Arabs—we hear them speaking in our own tongues the wonderful works of God." NKJV*

- Acts 10:46, *For they heard them speak with tongues and magnify God. NKJV*

- **Two types of tongues: (See Chapter 8, part 5 for more details on tongues)**

  - Tongues of man and of angels

    - *I Corinthians 13:1, Though I speak with the tongues of men and of angels, but have not love, I have become sounding brass or a clanging cymbal. NKJV*

    - You can pray in your earthly language (English, Spanish, etc)

    - You can pray in the language of the heavens, which would be tongues.

CHAPTER 3

Praise and Worship

Praise and worship have been greatly misunderstood in the church realm. When we say praise and worship, we immediately think of church and the worship team playing and singing during service.

Praise and worship do happen at church during the service, but this is NOT praise and worship, just another place it is supposed to be happening in our lives.

- ➤ PRAISE AND WORSHIP ARE A LIFESTYLE

  - o Praise and worship do not happen in just one location or when you have a band playing for you, it is an everyday experience that Jesus desires to introduce into your life.

  - o Praise and worship are not specifically surrounded with singing

  - o Praise and worship is an attitude and our life, not necessarily a song.

    - ▪ Romans 12:1, *I beseech you therefore, brethren, by the mercies of God, that you present your bodies a living sacrifice, holy, acceptable to God, which is your reasonable service. NKJV*

    - ▪ Praise and worship is our life. It is the sacrifice of our lives each day we live. Our goal should be to give Him glory and praise through our lifestyle.

    - ▪ Hebrews 13:15-16, *Therefore by Him let us continually offer the sacrifice of praise to God, that is, the fruit of our lips, giving thanks to His name. 16But do not forget to do good and to share, for with such sacrifices God is well pleased. NKJV*

    - ▪ The idea of the sacrifice when it comes to our lives is that it is the best, not the leftover. When we live for God and lay ourselves down, it is the first layer of praise and worship for our Father.

  - o Praise and worship is first an attitude that is manifest in the activity of praise and worship.

  - o Every day the greatest first step of becoming a worshiper is to offer yourself to Father as a living sacrifice and to give HIM your life for that day. Your very life is praise and worship to Daddy.

- ➤ THE HEART OF THE MATTER

- Praise and worship must also be established in your heart.

- It is not about the words you say or sing, but when you are living, speaking or singing, what is the heart saying?

- Is it just lips service or is it from your heart and you really mean what you are thinking, living and saying?

- When the heart is in the correct position, we again become praise and worship to our God.

  - John 4:21-24, *Jesus said to her, "Woman, believe Me, the hour is coming when you will neither on this mountain, nor in Jerusalem, worship the Father.* [22]*You worship what you do not know; we know what we worship, for salvation is of the Jews.* [23]*But the hour is coming, and now is,* **when the true worshipers will worship the Father in spirit and truth***; for the Father is seeking such to worship Him.* [24]*God is Spirit, and those who worship Him must worship in spirit and truth." NKJV*

➤ What is PRAISE?

- Praise and worship are not the same.

- Praise is thanking Him for what He has done.

  - Psalm 100:4-5, **Enter into His gates with thanksgiving, And into His courts with praise.** *Be thankful to Him, and bless His name.* [5] *For the Lord is good; His mercy is everlasting, And His truth endures to all generations. NKJV*

    - Thanksgiving

      - *Strongs Exhaustive Concordance # 8426 – Towdah is the Hebrew word. The definition - confession, praise, thanksgiving, give praise to God, thanksgiving in songs of liturgical worship, hymn of praise, thanksgiving choir or procession or line or company, thank-offering, sacrifice of thanksgiving confession. http://www.biblestudytools.com/lexicons/hebrew/kjv/towdah.html*

    - Praise

      - *Strongs Exhaustive Concordance # 8426 – Tahillah is the Hebrew word. The definition - praise, song or hymn of praise, praise, adoration, thanksgiving (paid to God) act of general or public praise. http://*

www.biblestudytools.com/lexicons/hebrew/kjv/ tehillah.html

- Understanding that when you are going to praise Him, you literally are coming into His presence and thanking Him for all that He has done in your life.

    o There are times that I break into praise when I am driving down the road, just thanking Jesus for my life and family.

    o There are times I am in the shower and just begin to thank God for a new day to be able to serve Him.

    o There are times that I start to praise when I see that He has protected me and worked in my life.

    o There are times that I break into praise and thanksgiving for something I have yet received, knowing that He will provide.

- Coming into God's presence is accomplished by beginning to praise and thank Him for what He has done in our lives.

- We all have something to thank and praise Daddy for. You might be going through a difficult time, but when you begin to praise Him you will see the power come down to meet that need.

    - Paul and Silas understood that principle

        o Acts 16:25-26, *But at midnight Paul and Silas were **praying and singing hymns to God**, and the prisoners were listening to them. 26Suddenly there was a great earthquake, so that the foundations of the prison were shaken; and immediately all the doors were opened and everyone's chains were loosed. NKJV*

- Verses that teach us to praise

    - Psalm 9:1, *I will praise You, O Lord, with my whole heart; I will tell of all Your marvelous works. NKJV*

        o *Strongs Exhaustive Concordance # 3034 – Yadah is another Hebrew word for praise. The definition is - to give thanks,, laud, praise, to confess, confess (the name of God) http://www.biblestudytools.com/ lexicons/hebrew/kjv/yadah.html*

- Psalm 35:28, *And my tongue shall speak of Your righteousness And of Your praise all the day long. NKJV*

  o Personal Praise

  - This is you individually everyday taking time to praise our Father for what He has done in our lives or what He will be doing in our lives.

  - When we do this we begin our day with focus and giving attention and thanks for the day ahead or in the midst of that day.

  - I would encourage you to start every day (that might take some self discipline) with praise. Either in the bed, shower, breakfast, car, wherever it might take place, you need to begin your day with surrender and praise to allow God to be our focus for the day ahead.

  o Public Praise

  - This is when a group of believers comes together in one place and gives thanks to the Father for what He has done individually and corporately.

    - Exodus 15:1-2, *Then Moses and the children of Israel sang this song to the Lord, and spoke, saying: "I will sing to the Lord, For He has triumphed gloriously! The horse and its rider He has thrown into the sea! 2 The Lord is my strength and song, And He has become my salvation; He is my God, and I will praise Him; My father's God, and I will exalt Him. NKJV*

    - Ezra 3:10-11, *When the builders laid the foundation of the temple of the Lord, the priests stood in their apparel with trumpets, and the Levites, the sons of Asaph, with cymbals, to praise the Lord, according to the ordinance of David king of Israel. 11And they sang responsively, praising and giving thanks to the Lord: "For He is good, For His mercy endures forever toward Israel." Then all the people shouted with a great shout, when they praised the Lord, because the foundation of the house of the Lord was laid. NKJV*

    - Psalm 22:25, *My praise shall be of You in the great assembly;.... NKJV*

    - Luke 19:34-38, *And they said, "The Lord has need of him." 35Then they brought him to Jesus. And they threw their own clothes on the colt, and they set Jesus on him. 36And as He went, many spread their clothes on the road. 37Then, as He was now drawing near the descent of the Mount of Olives, the whole multitude of the disciples began to rejoice and praise God with a loud voice for all the mighty works they had seen, [38]saying: "'Blessed is the King who comes in the name of the Lord!' Peace in heaven and glory in the highest!" NKJV*

- The corporate praise releases the blessing and power of God in a greater capacity because of the unity and synergy that is expelled.

- So do not just stand there during praise at church, get involved, it is Biblical and Father deserves it no matter what is happening in your life.

➤ WHAT IS WORSHIP?

o Worship is glorifying Him for who He is, not what He has done.

- I Chronicles 16:29, *Give to the Lord the glory due His name; Bring an offering, and come before Him. Oh, worship the Lord in the beauty of holiness! NKJV*

  • Worship

    o *Strongs Exhaustive Concordance # 7812 - Shachah is the Hebrew word. The definition - to bow down, prostrate oneself before superior in homage before God in worship*

- Psalm 95:6, *Oh come, let us worship and bow down; Let us kneel before the Lord our Maker. NKJV*

- John 4:24, *God is Spirit, and those who worship Him must worship in spirit and truth." NKJV*

o When we worship we focus on who He is as God, but also who He is to us.

- He is the Creator

- He is the King of kings

- He is the Lord of Lords

- He is the Alpha and Omega

- He is the Beginning and the End

- He is the Provider

- He is the Healer

- He is the Protector

- He is our Peace

- He is our Shepherd and Guide

- He is our Righteousness

- He is Faithful

- He is our Salvation

- He is our Deliverer

- He is our Friend

- He is our Daddy

- He is LOVE

- The list goes on and on and on

- He is the I AM, THAT I AM!

➢ POSITIONS AND MANIFESTATIONS OF PRAISE AND WORSHIP

- ○ The greatest position as explained in the beginning of the chapter is the position of the heart.

  - Your heart and focus must be correct

  - The people that take the Lord's name in vain more than any sinner are usually in the church. Taking the Lord's name is vain means that it is spoken without meaning or purpose. When we are in church during praise and worship and are just singing words, we are taking the Lord's name in vain.

  - A true worshiper is one who worships in spirit and in truth.

- ○ There are many physical positions and actions that are communicated in the Word for praise and worship.

  - Instruments playing

    - Psalm 150, *Praise the Lord! Praise God in His sanctuary; Praise Him in His mighty firmament! 2Praise Him for His mighty acts; Praise Him according to His excellent greatness! 3 Praise Him with the sound of the trumpet; Praise Him with the lute and harp! 4 Praise Him with the timbrel and dance; Praise Him with stringed instruments and flutes! 5 Praise Him with loud cymbals; Praise Him with clashing cymbals!* *6* *Let everything that has breath praise the Lord. Praise the Lord! NKJV*

- Singing aloud

  - Psalm 149:1, *Praise the Lord! Sing to the Lord a new song, And His praise in the assembly of saints. NKJV*

- Raising your hands

  - This one is misunderstood by most visitors and freaks them out. If I took a gun and put it to your chest and said, "stick'em up, give me all your money", you would raise your hands in surrender.

  - Raising your hands is simply an outward expression of what you are doing in your heart.

    - 1 Timothy 2:8, *I desire therefore that the men pray everywhere, lifting up holy hands, without wrath and doubting; NKJV*

    - Psalm 63:3-4, *Because Your lovingkindness is better than life, My lips shall praise You.* *4* *Thus I will bless You while I live; I will lift up my hands in Your name. NKJV*

- Shouting

  - The shout releases and breaks restraints and inhibitions. It is liberating!

    - Psalm 100:1, *Make a joyful shout to the Lord, all you lands! NKJV*

- Clapping your hands

  - Even if you do not have rhythm, it is for Jesus.

    - Psalm 47:1, *Oh, clap your hands, all you peoples! Shout to God with the voice of triumph! NKJV*

- Dancing before the Lord

  - This is one that really sends the panic buttons to the highest level.

  - Think about it though. When you were not serving Jesus you would dance with the opposite sex – getting your groove on! When you were in the bar you would dance yourself stupid.

- Why would we be ashamed to dance before the Lord our Maker?

- Why is it considered strange?

  - David danced before the Lord because he was so excited that the presence of the Lord returned to Israel.

    - 2 Samuel 6:14-15, *Then David danced before the Lord with all his might; and David was wearing a linen ephod. 15So David and all the house of Israel brought up the ark of the Lord with shouting and with the sound of the trumpet. NKJV*

  - Psalm 150:4, *Praise Him with the timbrel and dance; ...... NKJV*

- I don't do it often but when I do, it is the most liberating, free experience that breaks any care of what others think. It is a powerful rush to give Him everything and not care what others are feeling.

- Isn't it about time to be free!!!

- The new song

  - This is when from your innermost belly you just start praising and worshiping Him. There is no specific song you are singing, it is just erupting from your heart.

    - Psalm 98:1, *Oh, sing to the Lord a new song! For He has done marvelous things; His right hand and His holy arm have gained Him the victory. NKJV*

    - Psalm 33:3, *Sing to Him a new song; Play skillfully with a shout of joy. NKJV*

- The Glory Cloud

  - 2 Chronicles 5:13-14, *indeed it came to pass, when the trumpeters and singers were as one, to make one sound to be heard in praising and thanking the Lord, and when they lifted up their voice with the trumpets and cymbals and instruments of music, and praised the Lord, saying: "For He is good, For His mercy endures forever," that the house, the house of the Lord, was filled with a cloud, ¹⁴so that the priests could not continue ministering because of the cloud; for the glory of the Lord filled the house of God. NKJV*

- This is when the presence of the Lord so fills the place of worship that a cloud literally will descend and fill the room. It is tangible and weighty. Usually, nothing can be done when the glory of God fills a room. The response is simply to 'be' before Him. Some kneel, some lay prostrate, some just sit in silence before the King of the Universe. This is an amazing experience that cannot ever be forgotten.

➤ THE FINAL PURPOSE

- ○ Praise and worship is not about us, or using our skill before the Lord. If it becomes this, then our hearts are not focused or aimed toward Jesus.

- ○ It is all about the HEART, not the position of your body.

   - ▪ John 4:23-24, *But the hour is coming, and now is, when the true worshipers will worship the Father in spirit and truth; for the Father is seeking such to worship Him. ²⁴God is Spirit, and those who worship Him must worship in spirit and truth." NKJV*

CHAPTER 4

Repentance and Faith

Hebrews 6:1-2
Therefore, leaving the discussion of the elementary principles of Christ, let us go on to perfection, not laying again the foundation of repentance from dead works and of faith toward God, ²of the doctrine of baptisms, of laying on of hands, of resurrection of the dead, and of eternal judgment. NKJV

- ➢ **Not laying again the foundation of repentance**

    - ○ This verse sounds easy, but truthfully it is a serious problem in Christiandom.

        - ▪ Many Christians start well, but starting is not the end of it all. It is not how you start, but how you end!

    - ○ The foundation is imperative for success. Not just laying the foundation, but knowing that once you start building upon it, you should not have to go back and lift the building off the foundation to rebuild all over again.

        - ▪ I have watched many people receive Jesus as their Savior and get all excited, but just as the parable of the sower and the seed (Matthew 13:18-23) says, they walk away. Then like the prodigal son (Luke 15:11-24), they come to themselves and come home again.

            - • That is not the best way to live for the Lord, but I have watched people do that time and time and time and time and time and time and time…….. get the point?

            - • Jesus established these principles so that once you have learned them, you do not have to keep walking away and starting over. Lay the foundation ONCE, and then build! Walk with Jesus on that foundation and never have to lay it again.

    - ○ **"Not laying again"**

        - ▪ This also shows that there is a ton more for you to know and learn in Christ beyond salvation!

        - ▪ Many people come up front and ask Jesus into their hearts with sincerity. They truly desire Jesus, but that is as far as they go.

- God's desire is not for people to use Jesus as their get out of hell free card, but for Jesus to establish you in your destiny.

- Jesus did not save us just to go to heaven. If this was true then you would die or be raptured the moment you asked Him into your life.

- He saved you because you have purpose and destiny to complete while you are here.

■ Make a decision when you receive Jesus that you are never going back to the world. There is no place to go back to. It is all or nothing!

- Luke 9:62, *But Jesus said to him, "No one, having put his hand to the plow, and looking back, is fit for the kingdom of God." NKJV*

➢ **Repentance from dead works**

o Repentance

■ The word repentance means to turn 180 degrees from one direction to another.

■ To not return to the old mess.

■ 2 Corinthians 7:10, *For godly sorrow produces repentance leading to salvation, not to be regretted; but the sorrow of the world produces death. NKJV*

- Repentance is not, "I am sorry"

- Repentance is not, "I got caught"

- Repentance is when you realize you have hurt the One you love the most.

  o I usually ask for a husband and wife that I know love each other and have been married for a long time to stand up. After they stand up I have them face each other and give each other a kiss. I then tell the husband to punch his wife in the face! The man says NO! (I wonder at times if he is just afraid of his wife, I would be) I ask why he will not punch her and his response is that he loves his wife and does not want to hurt her.

  o That is the same principle of repentance. It is not that we are afraid to go to the Lake of Fire, or "oops, I got caught!" It is "I do not want to hurt Father God, the One I love the most".

- ○ When it is not that valued, then we can slip into legalism, which is obedience because we have to, not out of relationship.

- ○ This is a relationship, not a religion

➢ **Dead Works**

- ○ Dead works are when we try to do something to gain something.

- ○ You do this for me, and I will do this for you.

  - ▪ Salvation does not come because you and I are good enough.

  - ▪ We cannot ever be "good" enough for God.

  - ▪ In fact, God cannot love you anymore now that you are saved than before you are saved.

    - • You can please Him more, but He cannot love you more!

  - ▪ God's love is unconditional.

    - • That means He loves us the same all the time.

    - • That doesn't mean that He is always pleased with us, or even accepts us in our position, but He loves us without reservation.

    - • This is why He sent Jesus. He loves us so much that He wills that nobody perishes.

      - ○ 2 Peter 3:9, *The Lord is not slack concerning His promise, as some count slackness, but is longsuffering toward us, **not willing that any should perish but that all should come to repentance**. NKJV*

      - ○ John 3:15-17

- ○ This was a real factor in the book of Galatians.

  - ▪ Paul had gone in and preached Jesus and that you do not have to follow a bunch of "do's and don'ts", but that you simply need to ask Jesus into your life, He will wash away your sins and make you a new person.

- Ephesians 2:8-9, *For by grace you have been saved through faith, and that not of yourselves; it is the gift of God, 9not of works, lest anyone should boast. NKJV*

- Paul had established the same principles of salvation through faith and grace in Galatia. Those who pushed the Jewish law came in and said that they needed to receive Jesus, but they also had to follow all the laws of the Jewish customs.

  o This made Paul very mad and this was his response:

    ▪ Galatians 1:6-9, *I marvel that you are turning away so soon from Him who called you in the grace of Christ, to a different gospel, 7which is not another; but there are some who trouble you and want to pervert the gospel of Christ. 8But even if we, or an angel from heaven, preach any other gospel to you than what we have preached to you, let him be accursed. 9As we have said before, so now I say again, if anyone preaches any other gospel to you than what you have received, let him be accursed. NKJV*

    ▪ Let them be cursed with a curse!

    ▪ He said this because they were adding to what someone had to do to be saved.

  o What to guard yourself concerning?

    ▪ Do not allow you relationship to turn into a religion.

    ▪ I have found over the years that those who have been saved for a long time forget that this is not about doing all the right things, but doing them for the right reasons, and allowing people to grow as they are learning.

➢ Faith Toward God

  o What is FAITH?

    ▪ God is not moved by our needs

    ▪ God is not moved by our HOPE (hope is futuristic)

    ▪ God is moved by FAITH!

      • The word faith is synonymous with the word TRUST.

- The more we know Him the more we TRUST or have FAITH in Him.

- We can actually believe that what God says He can do, He will do!

- Faith is believing in something you cannot see or touch in this tangible world, yet already having obtained it.

  - Hebrews 11:1, *Now faith is the substance of things hoped for, the evidence of things not seen. 2For by it the elders obtained a good testimony. NKJV*

  - Hebrews 11:1, *NOW FAITH is the assurance (the confirmation, [a]the title deed) of the things [we] hope for, being the proof of things [we] do not see and the conviction of their reality [faith perceiving as real fact what is not revealed to the senses]. AMPLIFIED VERSION*

    o Faith is believing you have received it before it is physically touchable.

    o Today's "church" world says, "I'll believe it when I see it", that is not faith at all.

  - Romans 4:17b, *God, who gives life to the dead and calls those things which do not exist as though they did; NKJV*

  - Romans 1:17, *For in it the righteousness of God is revealed from faith to faith; as it is written, "The just shall live by faith." NKJV*

- Faith can be measured and increased

  - Jesus showed that faith can grow and be measured

    o A measure of faith has been given to everyone.

      - Romans 12:3, *For I say, through the grace given to me, to everyone who is among you, not to think of himself more highly than he ought to think, but to think soberly, as **God has dealt to each one a measure of faith**. NKJV*

    o Faith can be little.

      - Matthew 6:30, *Now if God so clothes the grass of the field, which today is, and tomorrow is thrown into the oven, will He not much more clothe you, O you of **little faith**? NKJV*

- Matthew 8:26, *But He said to them, "Why are you fearful, **O you of little faith**?" Then He arose and rebuked the winds and the sea, and there was a great calm. NKJV*

  o Faith can be increased.

  - Luke 17:5, *And the apostles said to the Lord, "**Increase our faith**." NKJV*

  o Faith can be GREAT.

  - Luke 7:9, *When Jesus heard these things, He marveled at him, and turned around and said to the crowd that followed Him, "I say to you, I have not found **such great faith**, not even in Israel!" NKJV*

  - Acts 6:8, *And Stephen, **full of faith** and power, did great wonders and signs among the people. NKJV*

  o Faith can be seen.

  - Luke 5:20, ***When He saw their faith**, He said to him, "Man, your sins are forgiven you." NKJV*

- How do I increase my faith?

  - Faith is increased when we get into His Word.

  - The more you are in His Word the more FAITH you will have.

    o Romans 10:17, *So then faith comes by hearing, and hearing by the word of God. NKJV*

  - This is why the devil works so hard to steal the Word from you. Satan strives to get you to miss church or skip catechism, because he knows that the more you know the Word and hear the Word the stronger you are going to be in FAITH toward Father God, and that you will believe in His Word.

  - Prepare you heart when you are hearing and reading the Word of God and make sure it is going on good ground and it will increase 30, 60, 100 fold.

    o Matthew 13:18-23

- Be faithful daily to read the Word.

  - If you are not good at reading get the Bible on CD and listen to it in your vehicle. Get the Word in you spirit and grow!

- The opposite of faith is doubt

  - Doubt says that God says He is able, but I do not believe that He really can do it.

  - Doubt is actually saying that God's Word is not true.

  - Doubt is the cancelation seal of faith, it is the opposite of faith.

  - Doubt has stolen so much from the saints of old and the saints even of today.

    - Doubt kept the children of Israel from entering into the Promised Land

      - Hebrews 3:18-19, *And to whom did He swear that they would not enter His rest, but to those who did not obey?* *19So we see that* **they could not enter in because of unbelief.** *NKJV*

      - Matthew 13:57-58, *But Jesus said to them, "A prophet is not without honor except in his own country and in his own house."* *58* **Now He did not do many mighty works there because of their unbelief.** *NKJV*

    - Doubt steals the Word through circumstances and natural events.

      - Matthew 14:29-32, *So He said, "Come." And when Peter had come down out of the boat, he walked on the water to go to Jesus.* *30But when he saw that the wind was boisterous, he was afraid; and beginning to sink he cried out, saying, "Lord, save me!"31And immediately Jesus stretched out His hand and caught him, and said to him, "O you of little faith, why did you doubt?"* *32And when they got into the boat, the wind ceased. NKJV*

        - When Peter walked to Jesus, he was not really walking on the water, he was walking on the Word of Jesus, COME.

- When he took his eyes off Jesus and allowed fear and doubt to overtake him he began to sink.

- Faith can be stolen because of life's circumstances, if you allow it.

- Speak the Word!

- Jesus is not asking you to deny the facts, but He is telling us to declare the TRUTH. The Word is Truth!

- John 8:31-32, *Then Jesus said to those Jews who believed Him, "If you abide in My word, you are My disciples indeed. 32And you shall know the truth, and the truth shall make you free." NKJV*

- When doubt comes and tries to steal the Word from your heart, take authority in the name of Jesus and tell the devil he is a liar!

  - Take authority over the thoughts in your mind and declare the Word over your circumstance.

    o 2 Corinthians 10:4-5, *For the weapons of our warfare are not carnal but mighty in God for pulling down strongholds, 5casting down arguments and every high thing that exalts itself against the knowledge of God,* ***bringing every thought into captivity to the obedience of Christ*** *NKJV*

CHAPTER 5

Spiritual Authority

Many Christians become afraid whenever the topics of demons and Satan come up. In the last chapter we explored the reality that both the Godly and demonic spiritual worlds are very active. When we look at this activity without knowing that we are safe as God's children, then fear is created. God is not into fear!

1 John 4:18, *There is no fear in love; but perfect love casts out fear, because fear involves torment. But he who fears has not been made perfect in love. NKJV*

In Jesus there is no need to fear Satan, demons or evil!

Let's prove it with the Word.

- ➢ Divine Authority

  - ○ As was stated in the last chapter that there is no battle between Daddy and Satan.

  - ○ Father God has Divine Authority, Ultimate, Unquestionable, Supernatural, Supremacy over Satan and any of his cohorts. There is no comparison! Satan is in a war for people, not against God as an individual.

- ➢ Understanding authority

  - ○ There has been a huge attack on authority. The reason for such a massive attack on authority is because when the devil can cause rebellion and undermine authority then he has debilitated the church.

  - ○ Without the willingness to submit to authority, you will never be able to work with authority.

    - ▪ Rebellion is as the sin of witchcraft. This is the flavor of Satan.

      - • 1 Samuel 15:23a, *For rebellion is as the sin of witchcraft, And stubbornness is as iniquity and idolatry... NKJV*

    - ▪ Rebellion is the plan of the devil to destroy authority.

  - ○ So when we move under authority, and in authority, we are being backed by the one with the power.

    - ▪ "When Christian Herter was governor of Massachusetts, he was running hard for a second term in office. One day, after a busy morning chasing votes (and no lunch) he arrived at a church barbecue. It was late afternoon and Herter was famished. As Herter moved down the serving line, he held out his plate to the woman serving chicken. She put a piece on his plate and turned to the next person in line. "Excuse me," Governor Herter said, "do you mind if I have another piece of chicken?"

"Sorry," the woman told him. "I'm supposed to give one piece of chicken to each person."

"But I'm starved," the governor said.

"Sorry," the woman said again. "Only one to a customer."

Governor Herter was a modest and unassuming man, but he decided that this time he would throw a little weight around.

"Do you know who I am?" he said. "I am the governor of this state."

"Do you know who I am?" the woman said. "I'm the lady in charge of the chicken. Move along, mister."" *Bits & Pieces*, May 28, 1992, pp. 5-6.

- If I were to go to multi-billionaire's bank, stand in line for a teller, and when it was my turn ask for $1 million dollars from his account, the teller would say (politely, I hope), "Sir, I have no authority to give you those funds. I am sorry." But if I removed a check from my pocket signed by the billionaire himself, she would smile sweetly, excuse herself for a few minutes to make sure the check was authentic and verify my identity, and then give me $1 million in cash. The difference is in the authorization granted by the billionaire's signature, power to transfer funds "in his name."

o Jesus was very impressed when a man grasped this understanding of authority, and he was not even a Jew.

- Matthew 8:5-10, *Now when Jesus had entered Capernaum, a centurion came to Him, pleading with Him, ⁶saying, "Lord, my servant is lying at home paralyzed, dreadfully tormented." ⁷And Jesus said to him, "I will come and heal him." ⁸The centurion answered and said, "Lord, I am not worthy that You should come under my roof. But only speak a word, and my servant will be healed. ⁹**For I also am a man under authority**, having soldiers under me. And I say to this one, 'Go,' and he goes; and to another, 'Come,' and he comes; and to my servant, 'Do this,' and he does it." ¹⁰When Jesus heard it, He marveled, and said to those who followed, "Assuredly, I say to you, I have not found such great faith, not even in Israel! ¹¹And I say to you that many will come from east and west, and sit down with Abraham, Isaac, and Jacob in the kingdom of heaven. ¹²But the sons of the kingdom will be cast out into outer darkness. There will be weeping and gnashing of teeth." ¹³Then Jesus said to the centurion, "Go your way; and as you have believed, so let it be done for you." And his servant was healed that same hour. NKJV*

- There is always order when it comes to authority. This man was under authority and exercised what he was granted while under that authority. When he spoke, he spoke on behalf of his authority and the authority stood behind him with power.

    - This whole process is called the POWER OF ATTORNEY

        - To act on behalf of…

        - This is when you act in business or in a decision-making situation. You are that person who's name you are signing, with their authority. You are acting on behalf of them and with the same authority. You are essentially, THEM.

- Jesus did not come in His own authority, but in the authority and name of the Father

    o Jesus could not do miracles and have authority over devils because He was the Son of God, because then He could not pass on that authority to us.

    o He received this authority because He was anointed by the Spirit. He did no mighty miracles until He was anointed at His baptism.

        - Mark 1:9-12, *It came to pass in those days that Jesus came from Nazareth of Galilee, and was baptized by John in the Jordan.* [10]*And immediately, coming up from the water, He saw the heavens parting and the Spirit descending upon Him like a dove.* [11]*Then a voice came from heaven, "You are My beloved Son, in whom I am well pleased."* [12]*Immediately the Spirit drove Him into the wilderness. NKJV*

    o It was not till this time that Jesus entered into the ministry and moved in the authority from the One who sent Him.

        - Acts 10:38, *how God anointed Jesus of Nazareth with the Holy Spirit and with power, who went about doing good and healing all who were oppressed by the devil, for God was with Him. NKJV*

    o Jesus was given the right to act on behalf of the Father in heaven and that is the only reason that Jesus could accomplish what He did.

        - John 12:49, *For I have not spoken on My own authority; but the Father who sent Me gave Me a command, what I should say and what I should speak. NKJV*

- John 12:50, *And I know that His command is everlasting life. Therefore, whatever I speak, just as the Father has told Me, so I speak." NKJV*

- Matthew 28:18, *And Jesus came and spoke to them, saying, "All authority has been given to Me in heaven and on earth. NKJV*

- Mark 1:27-28, *Then they were all amazed, so that they questioned among themselves, saying, "What is this? What new doctrine is this? For with authority He commands even the unclean spirits, and they obey Him." 28And immediately His fame spread throughout all the region around Galilee. NKJV*

- John 5:26-27, *For as the Father has life in Himself, so He has granted the Son to have life in Himself, 27and has given Him authority to execute judgment also, because He is the Son of Man. NKJV*

➢ Jesus had to leave to be able to give us His authority.

   o It can be compared to running a relay race. Each person has a leg on the team, and until that person fulfills their leg and takes their hands off the baton, the next racer cannot begin.

      ■ Jesus knew that He had to go away to send the Holy Spirit and anoint more people with the power to fulfill the will of God.

   o Even before He was raised and handed the authority to the church, Jesus was empowering the disciples while walking with them on earth.

      ■ Luke 9:1-2, *Then He called His twelve disciples together and gave them power and authority over all demons, and to cure diseases. 2He sent them to preach the kingdom of God and to heal the sick. NKJV*

   o When Jesus rose from the dead He had a plan.

      ■ The Church in which He is the head!

      ■ We are His body and are called to be His hands, feet, mouth, and the manifestation of Him in order to show His love.

         • John 14:10-14, *Do you not believe that I am in the Father, and the Father in Me? The words that I speak to you I do not speak on My own authority; but the Father who dwells in Me does the works. 11Believe Me that I am in the Father and the Father in Me, or else believe Me for the sake of the works themselves. 12"**Most assuredly, I say to you, he who believes in Me, the works that I do he will do also; and*** *greater works than these he will do, because I go to My Father. 13And whatever you ask in My name, that I will do, that the Father may be glorified in the Son. 14If you ask anything in My name, I will do it. NKJV*

- Matthew 28:18-20, *And Jesus came and spoke to them, saying, "All authority has been given to Me in heaven and on earth. 19Go therefore and make disciples of all the nations, baptizing them in the name of the Father and of the Son and of the Holy Spirit, 20teaching them to observe all things that I have commanded you; and lo, I am with you always, even to the end of the age." Amen. NKJV*

- Mark 16:15-20, *And He said to them, "Go into all the world and preach the gospel to every creature. 16He who believes and is baptized will be saved; but he who does not believe will be condemned. 17And these signs will follow those who believe: In My name they will cast out demons; they will speak with new tongues; 18they will take up serpents; and if they drink anything deadly, it will by no means hurt them; they will lay hands on the sick, and they will recover." 19So then, after the Lord had spoken to them, He was received up into heaven, and sat down at the right hand of God. 20And they went out and preached everywhere, the Lord working with them and confirming the word through the accompanying signs. Amen. NKJV*

➢ So we have been granted authority from Jesus to work on the Father's behalf.

  ○ What does this mean when we are talking about devils and Satan?

   ▪ This means that every devil in hell is subject to you as a believer in the name of Jesus, even Satan himself is subject to you in Jesus name.

    • Luke 10:17-20, *Then the seventy returned with joy, saying, "Lord, even the demons are subject to us in Your name." 18And He said to them, "I saw Satan fall like lightning from heaven. 19Behold, **I give you the authority** to trample on serpents and scorpions, **and over all the power of the enemy,** and nothing shall by any means hurt you. 20Nevertheless do not rejoice in this, that the spirits are subject to you, but rather rejoice because your names are written in heaven." NKJV*

   ▪ So how do I deal with a demonic attack when it happens to me?

    • You have to take authority in the name of Jesus!

- Not in your name, or the name of the church, but in the name of Jesus.

  - ○ "In the name of Jesus I bind you devil and command you to stop your activity"

  - ○ Demons are like dogs and they will press the issue until they know you are serious, so don't give up and keep putting him in his spot in the name of Jesus.

- Remember, any time you see your health, wealth, or family being attacked, you can be sure that it is not God.

    - ▪ James 1:16, *Do not be deceived, my beloved brethren. 17Every good gift and every perfect gift is from above, and comes down from the Father of lights, with whom there is no variation or shadow of turning. NKJV*

    - ▪ James 1:13, *Let no one say when he is tempted, "I am tempted by God"; for God cannot be tempted by evil, nor does He Himself tempt anyone. NKJV*

  - ○ Identify that this is a demonic attack and take the authority that Jesus passed to you to accomplish your freedom and continued liberty.

CHAPTER 6

Spiritual Warfare

When I was a child there was an understanding created in my mind through the church that I grew up in. This understanding was not taught, the topic of spiritual warfare was never brought up, and the concept was simply how the people of the church lived. I really believed that there was a war between God and Satan and that it was a HUGE battle. I believed that Satan was almost as powerful as God Himself and that we needed to be afraid of Satan and the demons.

I remember being in church on a Sunday morning when I was a young double-digit aged child. The church was one of those old style buildings with hard wooden pews and high ceilings. When you said boo, it would echo through the sanctuary. The stained glass windows were massive and reached all the way to the top of the majestic, artistically designed building. One Sunday morning during a contemporary worship service the pipes began to make this banging noise that was so loud, it overpowered the music being played. It drew the attention of the few hundred people in the building. All of a sudden 5 or so rows ahead of me came this piercing scream that made every hair on my head, arm and even armpit stand straight up! This 4' 11" girl dropped to the floor and started moving like a snake on her stomach up the aisle of the church toward the front. I saw the ushers try to grab and restrain her and then watched them get thrown around like rag dolls. The next thing I heard was, "Get the children to the basement, get the children to the basement." They quickly moved all the children, including myself to the basement as they exorcised the demonic spirit that was in the young woman.

I have pondered that moment many times and early in the ministry realized that we were all afraid of demons. In fact, the more I pondered it I found it to be funny because they thought that by putting the children in the basement everything would be ok with the kids. Then I chuckled, as I knew that demons go through floors!

We really believed that there was warfare and that it was a battle for God to restrain Satan. We were afraid of the devil!

This chapter will break that foolish concept in the minds of the Saints, and show you the authority that Jesus has passed to each and every Christian on this planet.

This is the secret Satan does not want you to know!!

> ➢ THE SPIRIT REALM IN VERY REAL

- The realms of the spirit are more real than the chair you are sitting in right now.

- You cannot see it, nor physically touch it, but it has been around a lot longer than the chair and will be around for eternity after the chair you are sitting in has deteriorated.

- We tend to place more faith in what we can see than what we cannot see. The truth is, it should be the opposite.

  - 2 Corinthians 4:18, *while we do not look at the things which are seen, but at the things which are not seen. For the things which are seen are temporary, but the things which are not seen are eternal. NKJV*

  - 2 Corinthians 5:7, *For we walk by faith, not by sight. NKJV*

  - Joshua experienced this when they were getting ready to take Jericho. God instructed him not to look at what was in front of him (the massive walls), but to see what God was going to do – look into the Spirit.

    - Joshua 6:1-2, *Now Jericho was securely shut up because of the children of Israel; none went out, and none came in. 2And the Lord said to Joshua: "**See!** I have given Jericho into your hand, its king, and the mighty men of valor. NKJV*

    - God was having Joshua look into the real realm, the realm of the spirit where the future is just as real as the now.

  - Elisha was able to show his servant the reality of the spirit world.

    - The king of Syria was plotting and planning against the children of God. The prophet Elisha was able to see it the spirit and warn the king of Israel. The Syrian king was so mad because he knew someone was telling secrets and he was ready to kill the traitor. He called his servant and the servant told him that the prophet of God was revealing even the things talked about in his bedroom. The Syrian king sent his army to kill the prophet in Dothan. When Elisha's servant woke up in the morning, he walked out to clean up and there was the army of Syria to kill Elisha and of course, him. To say the least he was nervous. Elisha walked out and Gehazi was freaking out! Elisha looked at him and said:

      - 2 Kings 6:16-17, *So he answered, "Do not fear, for those who are with us are more than those who are with them." 17And Elisha prayed, and said, "Lord, I pray, **open his eyes that he may see**." Then the*

Lord opened the eyes of the young man, and he saw. And behold, the mountain was full of horses and chariots of fire all around Elisha. NKJV

- What Gehazi saw was what already existed in the spirit, he just could not see it. The eternal is more real than the natural, perishing world that we live in today.

➢ WHO ARE THE MAIN PLAYERS IN THE SPIRIT WORLD?

- There are only two main players.

  - God

    - Angels

  - Satan

    - Demons

- I was taught more by example than by the Word that there was a battle in the heavens between God and Satan and that it was a struggle in the spirit realm. God and Satan were fighting and we were always hoping that God would win.

- I've got AWESOME news for you! God is NOT fighting Satan! The only power that Satan had and/or has is what was given to him from God who created him.

- Jesus already came and defeated him completely and made an open show of him.

  - Colossians 2:15, *Having disarmed principalities and powers, He made a public spectacle of them, triumphing over them in it. NKJV*

➢ GOD

- See Chapter 1

  - God is Spirit

    - John 4:24, *God is Spirit, and those who worship Him must worship in spirit and truth." NKJV*

  - He is the King, even in the spirit realm

    - 1 Timothy 6:15-16, *which He will manifest in His own time, He who is the blessed and only Potentate, the King of kings and Lord of lords, [16]who alone has immortality, dwelling in unapproachable light, whom no man has seen or can see, to whom be honor and everlasting power. Amen. NKJV*

- God is not in battle with Satan because He is the King and Satan was created – he only has what was granted to him.

➢ ANGELS

o These are beings created by God to do work for the Kingdom of God.

- Angels have different responsibilities

  - Some only worship

    o Isaiah 6:2-3, *Above it stood seraphim; each one had six wings: with two he covered his face, with two he covered his feet, and with two he flew. ³And one cried to another and said:"Holy, holy, holy is the Lord of hosts; The whole earth is full of His glory!" NKJV*

  - Some for war

    o 2 Kings 6:16-17, *So he answered, "Do not fear, for those who are with us are more than those who are with them." ¹⁷And Elisha prayed, and said, "Lord, I pray, **open his eyes that he may see**." Then the **Lord opened the eyes of the young man, and he saw**. And behold, the mountain was full of horses and chariots of fire all around Elisha. NKJV*

  - Some to protect

    o Psalm 34:7, *The angel of the Lord encamps all around those who fear Him, And delivers them. NKJV*

  - Some to do ministry for the saints

    o Hebrews 1:14, *Are they not all ministering spirits sent forth to minister for those who will inherit salvation? NKJV*

  - They all have diverse jobs for the King

- Angels are not to be worshiped

  - There is a trend that exists that gives attention to angels, encourages angel worship, and praying to them. This is not a God thing! Angels are created beings and are not to be worshiped nor offered glory nor prayed to. The angel that enjoys that attention is Satan. He tried to lift himself up above God and wanted the worship of God. Angel worship is demonic and promotes supernatural activity as attention is given to the demonic realm. The demons would like to convince people to focus on them rather than Jesus.

- Angels are spirits and do not have a physical body, but can take on a body to do work for God.

  - Genesis 19:1a, *Now the two angels came to Sodom in the evening, and Lot was sitting in the gate of Sodom. NKJV*

  - Numbers 22:31, *Then the Lord opened Balaam's eyes, and he saw the Angel of the Lord standing in the way with His drawn sword in His hand; and he bowed his head and fell flat on his face. NKJV*

- Angels cannot reproduce

  - Mark 12:25, *For when they rise from the dead, they neither marry nor are given in marriage, but are like angels in heaven. NKJV*

- Angels do not die

  - Luke 20:36, *nor can they die anymore, for they are equal to the angels and are sons of God, being sons of the resurrection. NKJV*

➢ SATAN

  ○ Satan only ever tries to counterfeit what God the Father is doing.

  ○ He was one of the three arch angels:

  - Michael is the warring angel – a good angel, **not fallen.**

    - "Who is like God?" He is mentioned several times in Daniel (10:13, 21, 12:1), once in Jude (1:9).

    - Revelation 12:7-9, ***And war broke out in heaven: Michael and his angels fought with the dragon; and the dragon and his angels fought,*** *⁸but they did not prevail, nor was a place found for them in heaven any longer. ⁹So the great dragon was cast out, that serpent of old, called the Devil and Satan, who deceives the whole world; he was cast to the earth, and his angels were cast out with him. NKJV*

  - Gabriel is the messenger angel – a good angel, **not fallen.**

    - His name means "strong man of God" or "God is my strength." He is spoken of by name four times: twice to Daniel to interpret the meaning of his visions (Daniel 8-9), once to announce John the Baptist's birth to his father Zacharias (Luke 1:11-20), and once to announce the birth of Jesus to Mary (Luke 1:26-38).

- Lucifer was the angel over worship, he was worship – *fallen.*

  - Ezekiel 28:13-16, *You were in Eden, the garden of God; Every precious stone was your covering: The sardius, topaz, and diamond, Beryl, onyx, and jasper, Sapphire, turquoise, and emerald with gold.* **The workmanship of your timbrels and pipes was prepared for you on the day you were created.** *NKJV*

o Satan is a created being, an angel, he is not equal with God

o When Lucifer decided to try to take over God's position, he was cast down and cursed.

- Ezekiel 28:15-17, *You were perfect in your ways from the day you were created, Till iniquity was found in you. 16 "By the abundance of your trading You became filled with violence within, And you sinned;* **Therefore I cast you as a profane thing Out of the mountain of God**; *And I destroyed you, O covering cherub, From the midst of the fiery stones. 17 "Your heart was lifted up because of your beauty; You corrupted your wisdom for the sake of your splendor; I cast you to the ground, I laid you before kings, That they might gaze at you. NKJV*

- Isaiah 14:121-15, *Your pomp is brought down to Sheol, And the sound of your stringed instruments; The maggot is spread under you, And worms cover you.' 12 "How you are fallen from heaven, O Lucifer, son of the morning! How you are cut down to the ground You who weakened the nations! 13* **For you have said in your heart: 'I will ascend into heaven, I will exalt my throne above the stars of God**; *I will also sit on the mount of the congregation On the farthest sides of the north; 14 I will ascend above the heights of the clouds, I will be like the Most High.' 15 Yet you shall be brought down to Sheol, To the lowest depths of the Pit. NKJV*

- Luke 10:18-20, *And He said to them, "I saw Satan fall like lightning from heaven. 19Behold, I give you the authority to trample on serpents and scorpions, and over all the power of the enemy, and nothing shall by any means hurt you. 20Nevertheless do not rejoice in this, that the spirits are subject to you, but rather rejoice because your names are written in heaven." NKJV*

o Satan is not all knowing

- He cannot read your mind or thoughts

- He only knows what you tell him

○ Satan is not all powerful

- He can do the supernatural, but he has the same power as the rest of the angels

- As a believer he has no power over you, only what you give him.

- You have power over him

○ Satan can only be in one place at a time

- He cannot be at more than one location at a time.

- He cannot be tempting you and the president of the country at the same time

- He is only at one location at one time

○ Satan is always changing, lying and deceiving. He is not faithful, even to his followers.

- He is the father of lies

    • John 8:44, *You are of your father the devil, and the desires of your father you want to do. He was a murderer from the beginning, and does not stand in the truth, because there is no truth in him. When he speaks a lie, he speaks from his own resources, for he is a liar and the father of it. NKJV*

○ Satan has a specific passion

- John 10:10a, *The thief does not come except to steal, and to kill, and to destroy……. NKJV*

    • God is LOVE

    • Satan is HATE

        ○ He hates everything to do with humanity because we have been made in the image of the one he despises the most, God Himself

            - Genesis 1:26a, *Then God said, "Let Us make man in Our image, according to Our likeness; NKJV*

- He has no love or compassion for any human and his focus is to make sure as few people will have what he can never have again – being _accepted_ in the presence of God.

- Satan will always strive to steal what Jesus paid for on the cross
  - Your relationship with the Father
    - Your family
    - The body of Christ
  - Your health
    - Get you sick because Jesus paid for your healing
  - Your wealth
    - Keep you in poverty so you never trust God with the least, money
- Satan has titles that show his character
  - He is the god (little "g") of this world
    - 2 Corinthians 4:4, _In whom **the god of this world** hath blinded the minds of them which believe not, lest the light of the glorious gospel of Christ, who is the image of God, should shine unto them. KJV_
  - Prince of the earth and air
    - John 12:31, _"Now is the judgment of this world: now shall the prince of this world be cast out." KJV_
    - John 14:30, _Hereafter I will not talk much with you: for the prince of this world cometh, and hath nothing in me. " KJV_
    - John 16:11, _"Of judgment, because the prince of this world is judged. " KJV_
    - Ephesians 2:2, _In which you once walked according to the course of this world, according to the prince of the power of the air, the spirit who now works in the sons of disobedience, NKJV_

- Satan has the right to kill anyone who is not a believer. He is their god and he by nature is the murderer

    - Hebrews 2:14, *Inasmuch then as the children have partaken of flesh and blood, He Himself likewise shared in the same, that through death He might destroy him who had the power of death, that is, the devil, NKJV*

        - He does not have that power over a believer because our Messiah took from him the keys of death, hell and the grave.

            - Revelation 1:18, *I am He who lives, and was dead, and behold, I am alive forevermore. Amen. And I have the keys of Hades and of Death. NKJV*

- Satan is our adversary

    - 1 Peter 5:8-9a, *Be sober, be vigilant; because your adversary the devil walks about like a roaring lion, seeking whom he may devour. ⁹Resist him, steadfast in the faith, NKJV*

        - He is a defeated adversary for the believer

        - Toothless to the saints of God who understand their authority over the devil.

- Satan is the accuser of the saints

    - Revelation 12:10-11, *Then I heard a loud voice saying in heaven, "Now salvation, and strength, and the kingdom of our God, and the power of His Christ have come, for the accuser of our brethren, who accused them before our God day and night, has been cast down. ¹¹And they overcame him by the blood of the Lamb and by the word of their testimony, and they did not love their lives to the death. NKJV*

        - He accuses us, but usually uses each other to do his job.

        - This is why gossip is so satanic, it is the very nature of Satan being manifest.

- Satan is the angel of light

    - 2 Corinthians 11:14, *And no wonder! For Satan himself transforms himself into an angel of light. NKJV*

- He is a deceiver and will come into your life with good things and nice things, but his plot is to steal what Jesus already paid for and what is in your covenant.

  - These are just some of his names, names describe character.

- Satan has organized his demonic army

  - Ephesians 6:11-13, *Put on the whole armor of God, that you may be able to stand against the wiles of the devil. [12]For we do not wrestle against flesh and blood, but against principalities, against powers, against the rulers of the darkness of this age, against spiritual hosts of wickedness in the heavenly places. [13]Therefore take up the whole armor of God, that you may be able to withstand in the evil day, and having done all, to stand. NKJV*

    - The domain of Satan is organized for destruction. This is not a game.

    - There are ranks in the demonic realm to keep order and to divide work to keep focused.

      - Principalities – Greek means CHIEF

      - Powers – MAGISTRATE

      - Rulers of darkness – WORLD RULER

      - Spiritual Wickedness – SPIRITUAL PLOTS

  - Colossians 2:15, *Having disarmed principalities and powers, He made a public spectacle of them, triumphing over them in it. NKJV*

> DEMONS

- Demons were created as angels but decided to follow Satan when he was cast out of the heavens by God the Father.

  - Because Satan cannot be in more than one place at a time, when we are being spiritually attacked it is usually a demonic spirit.

- One third of the angels decided to follow Lucifer in the rebellion and were cast out of heaven

  - Revelation 12:4a, *His tail drew a third of the stars of heaven and threw them to the earth.... NKJV*

- They attack and try to destroy humanity, and keep them from the blood of Jesus.

  - There are many types of demons, different jobs in Satan's realm

- Demons that cause sickness

    - Blindness – Matthew 12:22, *Then one was brought to Him who was demon-possessed, blind and mute; and He healed him, so that the blind and mute man both spoke and saw. NKJV*

    - Deafness – Mark 9:25, *When Jesus saw that the people came running together, He rebuked the unclean spirit, saying to it, "Deaf and dumb spirit, I command you, come out of him and enter him no more!" NKJV*

    - Mute / no speech – Matthew 9:32-33, *As they went out, behold, they brought to Him a man, mute and demon-possessed. ³³And when the demon was cast out, the mute spoke. And the multitudes marveled, saying, "It was never seen like this in Israel!" NKJV*

    - Infirmities – Luke 13:11, *And behold, there was a woman who had a spirit of infirmity eighteen years, and was bent over and could in no way raise herself up. NKJV*

- Demons strive to get people to commit suicide

    - Mark 9:22, *And often he has thrown him both into the fire and into the water to destroy him. But if You can do anything, have compassion on us and help us." NKJV*

- Can cause mental illness

    - Luke 8:27, *And when He stepped out on the land, there met Him a certain man from the city who had demons for a long time. And he wore no clothes, nor did he live in a house but in the tombs. NKJV*

- Demons work in many different areas of people lives

    - Addictions

    - Sexual sin (porn, sex before marriage, adultery)

    - They push the cults and occult practices (false teaching, witchcraft and doctrines of demons)

        - 1 Timothy 4:1, *Now the Spirit expressly says that in latter times some will depart from the faith, giving heed to deceiving spirits and doctrines of demons, NKJV*

- o Divisions in the home and church

  - From the very beginning this is the very nature of Satan. He understands the power of agreement and will strive to destroy the power of the family through division.

  - He knows that every time there was great power revealed the people were of one heart and one mind.

    - Babel

    - Pentecost

  - He strives to do all he can do with his demonic spirits to cause friction and division within family units and churches.

- There are many other demonic spirits that are active on this planet. Just a reminder, these spirits are not actually named these things, but are actively involved in those actions within people's lives.

➢ The Occult

- o Knowing that the spiritual world is very real it is important not to dabble in areas that can put us in a bad spot.

  - There are certain things that you should never play with because you will give the devil a foothold in your life.

- o The occult is very real and people are flocking to it because it is real and it works.

  - **Psychics** are real and they do have the ability to tell you real facts.

    - Where are they getting their information?

      - o There are only two places to get information from the spiritual world.

        - God

        - Satan

      - o Psychics get their information from the demonic world. They will give credit to god (notice the small "g", but not to Jesus, because they are not hearing from heaven.

- ○ Because psychics are tapping the demonic world they are able to tell the past and present in amazing details because demons can see those things and experiences.

- ○ Psychics cannot tell your future because demons do not know the future. They will predict and when people hear it they will actually aim their life in that direction and make things happen themselves.

- Psychics are demonically based and you should never go to one, and if you have, you should renounce that demonic influence in your life.

- **They are not mediums** between you and your loved ones who have passed on into eternity.

  - ○ When a person dies they either enter heaven or enter hell. They do not come back or talk with the living.

  - ○ What was it then? I know it was my grandmother on the bottom of my bed, I saw her!

    - It was not your grandmother it was a FAMILIAR SPIRIT.

    - Ghosts – a ghost is not the soul of a person who is wandering the earth, it is a demon taking on the likeness of a human drawing attention to itself, and away from Jesus.

    - Deuteronomy 18:10-12, *There shall not be found among you anyone who makes his son or his daughter pass through the fire, or one who practices witchcraft, or a soothsayer, or one who interprets omens, or a sorcerer, [11]or one who conjures spells, or a medium, or a spiritist, or one who calls up the dead. [12]For all who do these things are an abomination to the Lord, and because of these abominations the Lord your God drives them out from before you. NKJV*

    - *Don't you dare sacrifice your son or daughter in the fire. Don't practice divination, sorcery, fortunetelling, witchery, [11]casting spells, holding séances, or channeling with the dead. [12]People who do these things are an abomination to God. It's because of just such abominable practices that God, your God, is driving these nations out before you. MESSAGE BIBLE*

- The demon has taken on the likeness of a human being, to lure you into communicating with the demonic side of the spirit world and take your eyes off Jesus.

- Demons just like angels. They can take on human likeness, but they are not that person.

- Demonically based groups

  - Wicca – worship the earth

  - Witches – no such thing as a Godly one

  - Warlocks – leaders in magic

  - New Age – beliefs entrenched in demonic activity

  - Reiki – demonic healers

  - Covens – groups of demonic believers

  - Eckankar – demonic soul travel

  - Santeria – Spanish witchcraft

  - Native American religion – they tap the spirit world

  - There are so many more

- Séances, palm reading, ouija boards, tarot cards, crystal balls, tea leaf reading, fortune telling, some music, spell casting, charms or tools for these activities, are all things you should not have or be involved in because it leaves the open door for demonic spirits in your life.

  - I remember getting a call from a man who was having things move around in his house and it was freaking him out! Lights coming on and off, things moving, footsteps in the residence, were all occurring. Some would say this was just a poltergeist (an active demon). I went down to the house to cast the demons out of the home and when I got there I saw a Native American medicine man stick. I looked at him and told him to move it to the shed and it would all stop. He moved it and all the demonic activity in the home ceased. Why? That stick was used for demonic activity and when you have those things dedicated to Satan in your house, it is the same as giving them the key to the front door for them to come in and play with you or even try to hurt you.

- This is not a game!

- Get rid of the things you have that would leave a front door key for the demonic to enter your home.

    o Acts 19:19-20, *Also, many of those who had practiced magic brought their books together and burned them in the sight of all. And they counted up the value of them, and it totaled fifty thousand pieces of silver. [20]So the word of the Lord grew mightily and prevailed. NKJV*

- Desensitization of our youth

    - There is a strong movement to desensitize our children from the demonic realm

        o TV shows/Movies

            ▪ Harry Potter (make magic and satanic activity fun)

            ▪ Charmed

            ▪ Twilight

        o Yu-Gi-Oh cards (Japanese religion and demonic)

        o Cartoons (spell casting, demons are normal)

        o Books

        o Video games (many are spell casting and fighting and or being demons)

        o Music

    - This is not to cause fear, but we are responsible for what we allow our children to feed their spirits with. Feed them Satan and don't be surprised when they reject God.

    o No need to fear, but we must be WISE.

➢ The next chapter deals with how you and I have authority over Satan and demons.

CHAPTER 7

Deliverance

2 Corinthians 4:18, **While we do not look at the things which are seen, but at the things which are not seen.** _**For the things which are seen are temporary, but the things which are not seen are eternal.**_ **NKJV**

By nature we as humans base the majority of our faith and understanding upon things that we can touch, smell, taste, see and hear. Because of that we have limited ourselves to the temporal aspects of reality.

What we cannot see is more real than what we can see!

The eternal always was and always will be; the chair you are sitting in or the car that you drive or house you live in will be gone in years to come.

As discussed in the last chapter on Spiritual Authority (chapter 14), we have that authority over the demonic world run by Satan.

In this chapter we will teach you how to cast out or off a devil so that you can be free or you can be used by the Holy Spirit to set someone free.

John 8:36,

Therefore if the Son makes you free, you shall be free indeed. NKJV

- ➤ OPPRESSION or POSSESSION
  - ○ There is a HUGE difference between the two and it is important to understand the difference if you are going to be free or be used in deliverance.
    - ▪ OPPRESSION
      - • This is when a demonic spirit is on someone (outside the body), but is not in them.
      - • Oppression is best understood as being lorded over, and controlled, but not being owned by that entity. Strongly influenced by that demon.
    - ▪ POSSESSION
      - • Possession means ownership. When a demon possesses a person, they literally own and live in and through that person.

- Demons come to counterfeit what God has done through His Son Jesus.

- Just as Jesus needs a body to live through, so too a demon needs a body to live through.

- When a person is possessed a demon comes in and lives in the soul of that individual.

➢ OPPRESSION

○ Number one thing to truth to grab a hold of is that a Christian CANNOT be demon possessed, but can be oppressed.

○ There is a fad that comes in and out of Christian society that says a Christian can be possessed. There was actually a church like that in our area for a bit. They would have the Christian sit in the middle of a ring of leaders and they would pray and the "Spirit" of God would tell them what demons the Christian had and then they would cast them out. It is a control issue! The pastor or church can control you as long as they have to keep delivering you from demonic spirits.

○ When I was at Bible College there was a student at the school who was telling other students that they were possessed and needed deliverance. They would have these "sessions" in his dorm room. There was even manifestations of demonic activity (when you give a demon a green light it will take full advantage). I confronted him and told him that if he continued, I would go to the dean and expose his false doctrine. He told me I was wrong, so I said get the Word out and I will too and whatever the Word declares, that is truth. I proved that the Spirit of God would not live in the same house as a demonic spirit. He ceased his activity.

  - 1 Corinthians 6:19-20, *Or do you not know that your body is the temple of the Holy Spirit who is in you, whom you have from God, and you are not your own?* *20For you were bought at a price; therefore glorify God in your body and in your spirit, which are God's.* NKJV

  - We as Christians are literally possessed by God's Spirit and He lives inside us and through us.

  - Colossians 1:27, *To them God willed to make known what are the riches of the glory of this mystery among the Gentiles: which is Christ in you, the hope of glory.* NKJV

  - Galatians 2:20, *I have been crucified with Christ; it is no longer I who live, but Christ lives in me; and the life which I now live in the flesh I live by faith in the Son of God, who loved me and gave Himself for me.* NKJV

- 1 John 4:4, *You are of God, little children, and have overcome them, because He who is in you is greater than he who is in the world. NKJV*

- God would never share His house with a demonic spirit.

- Mark 3:24-27, *If a kingdom is divided against itself, that kingdom cannot stand. 25And if a house is divided against itself, that house cannot stand. 26And if Satan has risen up against himself, and is divided, he cannot stand, but has an end. 27No one can enter a strong man's house and plunder his goods, unless he first binds the strong man. And then he will plunder his house. NKJV*

○ So a Christian can be demon <u>oppressed</u>. That means that a demon can come upon a Christian or latch a hold of a Christian, but cannot live within.

- A Christian who is oppressed can have a literal demon spirit sitting on their shoulder whispering in their ear.

  • When I was in Bible College we had a weekend that Pastors brought potential students from their churches to visit. A Pastor sat across from me at supper and in my spirit I could tell there was something wrong. I couldn't put my finger on it; I just knew something wasn't right with him. It seemed like everything that came out of his mouth was laced with something icky. Later that evening another student who was crisp with discernment of Spirits came to me and was sharing about a Pastor he saw that had a demon sitting on his shoulder and whispering in his ear. He described the guy, and it was the preacher who ate across from me at supper!

- Demons can latch onto a person and cause tormenting dreams and depression

  • There was a woman in Tennessee, while I was on the road, that was in the line for prayer on a Sunday night. When she got to me, she turned and ran out of the church and didn't come back till Wednesday night. I looked at her and saw 2 different spirits on her. A tormenting spirit and a depressive spirit. I just knew they were there, so I spoke to those devils and told them to come off her in Jesus name. Her face changed! She started dancing! She was free! Later she shared that when she was 4, she was raped and sexually abused and to stay safe she would talk to herself and communicate with herself. A demon saw this opening and latched a hold of her. She said that at nights, a little girl's voice (her voice) would talk with her out loud in her room and in her dreams. The Sunday night that she came for prayer that little girl's voice told her to run! After Wednesday night, it was running, because she was free! She was in her mid thirties.

- Demons can oppress with addictions

  - Romans 6:6, *knowing this, that our old man was crucified with Him, that the body of sin might be done away with, that we should no longer be slaves of sin. NKJV*

  - When you are born again, and you are driven beyond the normal fleshly desire, there is usually a demonic spirit behind that compulsion. We have all authority over our flesh, so the only sin we commit is when we yield to the desires of the flesh (James 1:12-15). When the temptation is driving beyond a normal fleshly temptation, then a demon is usually influencing you to commit the sin instead of living in freedom.

- Demons can oppress with sickness

  - Luke 13:11-13, 16, *And behold, there was a woman who had a spirit of infirmity eighteen years, and was bent over and could in no way raise herself up. 12But when Jesus saw her, He called her to Him and said to her, "Woman, you are loosed from your infirmity." 13And He laid His hands on her, and immediately she was made straight, and glorified God. 16So ought not this woman, being a daughter of Abraham, <u>whom Satan has bound</u>—think of it—for eighteen years, be loosed from this bond on the Sabbath?" NKJV*

  - I was in Maine preaching the Word and delivered a Word of Knowledge about a person with a specific pain in their lower back and that the Lord was going to heal them. The man came forward and I laid hands on his back and released the healing anointing. When I did that, the pain left that part of his back and went to his side. I prayed for his side and the pain went a little further toward the front. At that moment I knew it was a demon causing sickness. I spoke to that spirit to come off his body and he was completely healed at that moment.

- Demons can oppress with fear or phobia's

  - I was in Orange, Massachusetts preaching a revival and the power and presence of God was awesome. A woman came up to me at the end of one of the services and told be that she was going to try to bring a believer who had agoraphobia (that is a person who is afraid of crowds) for 5 years. She had not left her house for 5 years! They brought her in the next evening and she stayed in the back of the building. After service I had them bring her up and I cast that spirit of fear off her and immediately she was free and could go out and do anything she desired.

- 2 Timothy 1:7, *For God has not given us a spirit of fear, but of power and of love and of a sound mind. NKJV*

○ There are many more examples that can be communicated but let's cut to the chase.

  ▪ To get rid of demonic oppression is rather easy for a believer.

  ▪ As was explained in the last chapter about your authority as a child of God, demons are totally subject to you and know it. They just hope you do not figure this thing out.

  ▪ You do not pray a spirit off, you cast a spirit off!

  ▪ Speak to that demon and command it to go in Jesus name!

    - Luke 10:18-19, *Behold, I give you the authority to trample on serpents and scorpions, and over all the power of the enemy, and nothing shall by any means hurt you. 20Nevertheless do not rejoice in this, that the spirits are subject to you, but rather rejoice because your names are written in heaven." NKJV*

  ▪ Take authority over that spirit and command it to go, and it has to go.

  ▪ Demons are much like a dog

    - When you tell a dog to go and sit down, they might put up a fight, but you have to take authority or they will start running you. Even after the dog is sitting, most dogs will wait for you to forget or turn your head and they are heading back to where they were. Likewise, even though you cast an oppressive spirit off, you have to pay attention because it will try to come back and get what it desires (your liberty). Do not be surprised when you have to take authority more than once. Until they know that they are not getting back what they lost, they will keep trying. When they realize you are not leaving room for them and will not tolerate their presence, they will back off.

➤ POSSESSION

- This is a different beast all together. Possession is when the demon lives inside the soul of a person and is in control of that person.

- Jesus dealt with demon possession

  - Matthew 9:32-33, *As they went out, behold, they brought to Him a man, mute and demon-possessed. 33And when the demon was cast out, the mute spoke. And the multitudes marveled, saying, "It was never seen like this in Israel!" NKJV*

  - Matthew 17:14-21, *And when they had come to the multitude, a man came to Him, kneeling down to Him and saying, 15"Lord, have mercy on my son, for he is an epileptic and suffers severely; for he often falls into the fire and often into the water. 16So I brought him to Your disciples, but they could not cure him." 17Then Jesus answered and said, "O faithless and perverse generation, how long shall I be with you? How long shall I bear with you? Bring him here to Me." 18And Jesus rebuked the demon, and it came out of him; and the child was cured from that very hour. 19Then the disciples came to Jesus privately and said, "Why could we not cast it out?" 20So Jesus said to them, "Because of your unbelief; for assuredly, I say to you, if you have faith as a mustard seed, you will say to this mountain, 'Move from here to there,' and it will move; and nothing will be impossible for you. 21▪ However, this kind does not go out except by prayer and fasting." NKJV*

  - Mark 5:1-20, *Then they came to the other side of the sea, to the country of the Gadarenes. 2And when He had come out of the boat, immediately there met Him out of the tombs a man with an unclean spirit, 3who had his dwelling among the tombs; and no one could bind him, not even with chains, 4because he had often been bound with shackles and chains. And the chains had been pulled apart by him, and the shackles broken in pieces; neither could anyone tame him. 5And always, night and day, he was in the mountains and in the tombs, crying out and cutting himself with stones. 6When he saw Jesus from afar, he ran and worshiped Him. 7And he cried out with a loud voice and said, "What have I to do with You, Jesus, Son of the Most High God? I implore You by God that You do not torment me." 8For He said to him, "Come out of the man, unclean spirit!" 9Then He asked him, "What is your name?" And he answered, saying, "My name is Legion; for we are many." 10Also he begged Him earnestly that He would not send them out of the country. 11Now a large herd of swine was feeding there near the mountains. 12So all the demons begged Him, saying, "Send us to the swine, that we may enter them." 13And at once Jesus gave them permission. Then the unclean spirits went out and entered the swine (there were about two thousand); and the herd ran violently down the steep place into the sea, and drowned in the sea. ¹⁴So those who fed the swine fled, and they told it in the city and in the country. And they went out to see what it was that had happened. ¹⁵Then they came to Jesus, and saw the one who had been demon-possessed and had the legion, sitting and clothed and in his right mind. And they were afraid. ¹⁶And those who saw it told them how it happened to him who had been demon-possessed, and about the swine. ¹⁷Then they began to plead with Him to depart from their region. ¹⁸And when He got into the boat, he who had been demon-possessed begged Him that he might be with Him. ¹⁹However, Jesus did not permit him, but said to him, "Go home to your friends, and tell them what great things the Lord has done for you, and how He has had compassion on you." ²⁰And he departed and began to proclaim in Decapolis all that Jesus had done for him; and all marveled. NKJV*

- Acts 16:16-18, *Now it happened, as we went to prayer, that a certain slave girl possessed with a spirit of divination met us, who brought her masters much profit by fortune-telling. ¹⁷This girl followed Paul and us, and cried out, saying, "These men are the servants of the Most High God, who proclaim to us the way of salvation." ¹⁸And this she did for many days. But Paul, greatly annoyed, turned and said to the spirit, "I command you in the name of Jesus Christ to come out of her." And he came out that very hour. NKJV*

o There are many other references to a demon-possessed person being freed in the name of Jesus.

o How to cast out a devil

  - This is not a difficult thing for a believer. We have been mandated to cast out devils in the Word of God.

    • Mark 16:17a, *And these signs will follow those who believe: In My name they will cast out demons;.....NKJV*

  - We are able to do this in the NAME OF JESUS; not in our name or power. They were defeated by Jesus. We are just enjoying the empowerment from that victory.

  - Knowing Jesus and not just using His name is important.

  - Acts 19:13-16, *Then some of the itinerant Jewish exorcists took it upon themselves to call the name of the Lord Jesus over those who had evil spirits, saying, "We exorcise you by the Jesus whom Paul preaches." ¹⁴Also there were seven sons of Sceva, a Jewish chief priest, who did so. ¹⁵And the evil spirit answered and said, "Jesus know, and Paul I know; but who are you?"* [16] *Then the man in whom the evil spirit was leaped on them, overpowered them, and prevailed against them, so that they fled out of that house naked and wounded. NKJV*